Defund D.O.C:
Turning All Prisons Into Treatment and Career Centers

Daniel Simms

Cadmus Publishing
www.cadmuspublishing.com

Copyright © 2022 Daniel Simms

Cover art by Tad M. Bomboli

Published by Cadmus Publishing LLC

www.cadmuspublishing.com

Haledon, NJ

ISBN: 978-1-63751-523-5

All rights reserved. Copyright under Berne Copyright Convention, Universal Copyright Convention, and Pan-American Copyright Convention. No part of this book may be reproduced, stored in a retrieval system, or transmitted in any form, or by any means, electronic, mechanical, photocopying, recording or otherwise, without prior permission of the author.

Table of Contents

Foreword	1
Introduction	5
Discipline Without Love is Tyranny	9
Let Us End All Vestiges of Slavery	13
Repeal Victimless Crimes and All Enhancements	17
Restore Voting Rights To All Incarcerated Americans	21
Abolish Over-Sentencing!	25
Stop All Forms of Exploitation	29
Abolish All Forms of Oppression	33
Mandate Mental Health Treatment to End Recidivism	37
Mandate Education and Careers to End Recidivism	41
Tear Down Prison Walls and Begin Socialization Efforts	45
End Solitary Confinement, Diesel Treatment, and Cell Insecurity	49
Conclusion	53
Acknowledgment	57

Foreword

First and foremost you should know that this book is being written by an ultimate Stakeholder. I have experienced the criminal justice system continually nonstop since the age of thirteen years old. Before that I was in foster care but that story is told in the book "Hopeless in Seattle: A Fosterkid's Manifesto." This book, however, is written with first hand knowledge of what is happening in the criminal justice system, what is going wrong, and what we can do to fix it. It is that simple. Of course it may be hard for some to take this book serious as it is written by an uneducated incarcerated individual. Indeed my last grade of formal education was the sixth grade but I can assure you I have a doctorate degree in guard brutality, prison administration corruption, prison profiteering, injustices, and inhumane prison conditions. As I've experienced those for years. Being State raised in the juvenile and adult prison system provides me with a birds eye view and the opportunity to share my unique perspective and point of view in an attempt to better it for all future Americans. I have the credibility and standing to express my experiences and my suggested remedies better than most anyone else. What I see and hear within these prison walls is intentionally kept hidden from the outside world. But not anymore. I plan on revealing the true state of the criminal justice system. How it exploits and oppresses Americans with impunity. How it systematically creates new victims by releasing mentally ill, poor, antisocial, and uneducated peoples into society.

Seeing these atrocities on a daily basis gives me the credibility to boldly speak the truth. And the truth is, there is a stain on this country and it is known worldwide as mass incarceration. The land of the free has become the land of suffering and exploitation of its own people. To be sure, crime has to be addressed in any society, but in this advanced civilized country it is abhorrent to witness such backward, inequitable, and oppressive treatment. There are better answers. And believe it or not those answers can come from stakeholders educated by the Universities of Systemic Oppression. Yes I mean prisoners or ex-prisoners. They are a untapped resource that could be used to dramatically lower crime, reduce huge debt loads to fund prisons, and release immensely productive citizens at the same time. Using common sense approaches that are guaranteed to work! Yes guaranteed! This is not bluster. Hyperbole. Or outlandish theories. This is true knowledge, experience, and wisdom distilled from hours, days, weeks, months, years, and decades of governmental control and custody. Seeing that up close and personal for so long has made me an expert and trusted hand in conveying the hard truths and shocking revelations told herein.

Many times throughout my journey I have met many different types of peoples. Just like any one else has in their life. The noticeable difference, however, is that the people I have interacted with on a grand scale is murderers, shooters, robbers, gang members, drug addicts, and many other colorful peoples. But the most cutthroat and unforgiving peoples I've had experience with is the guards, prison administration, pro-prison politicians, prison profiteers, and other self-interested individuals intent on perpetuating this fraud known as mass incarceration on the American people. Sure its nice to put away troubled Americans when they commit crime, but it should also be equally nice to know that those "put away" are not becoming worse than when they went in. That is the case today. We can have a frank conversation in this country about where we want to be one hundred years from now. What we want our children's children to experience when they interact with the criminal justice system. That conversation is long overdue. Let those with bachelors, doctorates, and masters degrees be enlightened by a uneducated incarcerated, or ex-incarcerated, American citizen that has been through the struggle firsthand for decades. Through the pressure on all sides. Dealing with daily violence, gangs, and prison politics, only to turn around and have brutal guards suppress me, corrupt prison administrators abuse their power with overly harsh and petty rules and regulations meant to harass and keep me down. Then when those struggles and pressures have gotten so extreme that only family, friends, and community can cure them, prison profiteers keep you separated from them by their exorbitantly high priced and overly restrictive communication regime. It is a crazy and hostile environment. A world where only the strong can survive for decades. And this is the world I am in as we speak. But even if I was freed tomorrow, I would still articulate and express this struggle, because this struggle is an American experience that should be talked about and debated.

Most books on the topic discussed herein are written, published, marketed, and advertised by like minded individuals intent on addressing social justice issues. The same is true for this book. It is not meant to harass authority but to pressure it the same way I have been pressured by the evils of mass incarceration. Raising new ideas and destroying failing ones is part of the human and American experience. And as a human and American willing to share my perspective based on my experiences we should all collectively sit around the coffee table of shared humanity and citizenship to explore new ideas to improve America for all people. Not just the wealthy, privileged, and powerful. We can endeavor and strive together to make the criminal justice system a resounding success that countries around the world lift up and talk positively about, rather than look at with disdain and disbelief, that is possible. Even uneducated peoples can see that. It is readily apparent and self evident. That is clear.

Introduction

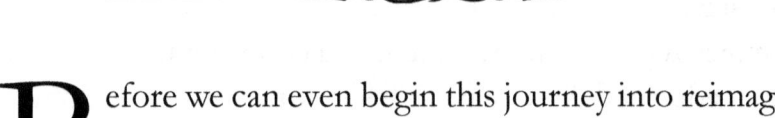

Before we can even begin this journey into reimagining a more civilized and fair criminal justice system we have to realize two fundamental facts: (1) the vast majority of those incarcerated will be released back into our society one day and (2) most are fellow Americans. Those two facts alone justify reimagining the system used today to incarcerate the American people. America needs a criminal justice system that encourages rehabilitation, treatment of mental health disorders, instills prosocial behaviors, and promotes self-sustainability through educational and career development. Currently America has a failing prison system that warehouses its people, ignores mental health illnesses, breeds antisocial behavior, and releases Americans uneducated, poor, and without any career prospects. This unsurprisingly results in Americans returning to the exact same negative lifestyle they had before incarceration. So upon their release a whole new set of victims is created.

The pro-prison media, pro-prison government officials, Democrat and Republican, corrupt prison administrators, and prison profiteers would like the public to narrow mindedly blame and severely punish the mentally disturbed, poor, uneducated, and jobless for returning to their troubled ways. Yet it is the pro-prison special interests that should be blamed for the new victims as they are prepetuating a known failed system that creates those victims. Prison administrators have a duty to correct and rehabilitate Americans but they are negligent in that duty. They have a vested interest in keeping prisons full. If they were to treat, educate, and provide career training those American citizens would be released pro-social, productive, and ready to start their careers. The recidivism cycle would be broken, families repaired and reunited, and communities strengthened with educated Americans. This is common sense. So why is it that prison special interests are so against this approach? It is because whole industries have sprouted around prisons. Its all about the money. It isn't about public safety, correction, or rehabilitation. Therefore we as the American people have to call for change. For a reimagining to a more humane, civilized, and evidence based criminal justice system. It will be hard no doubt because prison special interests are entrenched in media, government, and private industries but it can happen. If one State follows this manual and proves it successful then other States will eventually enact similar criminal justice reforms. As a native Washingtonian I hope my State will be the first to enact similar reforms. Seeing any State do so will be a blessing. The struggle for equality and a more perfect union is universal. Every people of every country seeks the best way to adjudge their populations for crimes and discipline them fairly according to their customs and practices. We should not be afraid in this country to envision a better criminal justice system either. The experiment of American extends to the experiment of mass incarceration. And that system has exceeded its life cycle. It has repeatedly produced worse Americans than have gone in. It is no longer feasible to blame the incarcerated American for recidivism. That blame now lays squarely on this corruptible system of mass incarceration. Keeping Americans caged, warehoused, oppressed and exploited, the government has been derelict in their duties. Every prison across this country should go into receivership. Into the hands of administrators with peace, good will, and harmony for all Americans in their custody and control. Administrators willing to treat incarcerated Americans as human beings worthy of redemption, restoration, and rehabilitation. Reform minded individuals must be stakeholders. Someone that has experienced the heavy hand of the government on their family, friend, or community member. Maybe then the top down reformation of equality and justice can begin to invade the desolate and dark reaches of the darkest prisons across this country.

In essence this book seeks to offer, extend, and propagate the message of hope, forgiveness, restoration, rehabilitation, and reentry. As a country and a people it is incumbent to reign in unjust and culturally repulsive laws, systems, and practices that no longer advance the human condition. Laws that offer the illusion or appearance of justice should be abolished. Some of these injustices, oppressive laws, systems, and practices are delineated in the preceding chapters. Obviously not all can be adequately addressed in one volume. But highlighting the most egregious and backward policies, practices, patterns, or maltreatments can shed light on the rampant guard brutality, corrupt prison administrators, vicious and exploitative prison profiteers, stolen slave labor/energy practices, blatantly harsh disenfranchisement voting laws, cruelly over-sentencing Americans, intentionally keeping incarcerated Americans untreated, stupid, and careerless so they recidivate within three years each will be addressed thoroughly and passionately herein to culminate into a small American opus future generations may reflect upon to discuss the American struggle of the oppressed American peoples stuck in the cycle of recidivism. We are not foreigners incarcerated in these American prisons, we are fellow Americans, nevertheless we are treated harshly, unfairly, even cruelly. I do not say this to pass judgment but merely to make this a more perfect union. To hark the same Patriotic yell that Paul Revere did when change was demanded by the people. The American people are ready for such change today. Mass incarceration is a scourge and plague on this country. It is time to examine different approaches to criminal justice. To approach it with heart, understanding, logic, and reason. Based on data. Evidence. And incontrovertible truths such as shared humanity, forgiveness, love, and progress.

Chapter One

Discipline Without Love is Tyranny

Are we punishing, getting revenge, seeking retribution, or disciplining our American people? That is the question. And if we are trying to discipline our people, just like you would discipline your child, then we need to approach it with love and compassion, just like we would with our own children. Yet many Americans have profoundly concluded that this country's criminal justice system has become a horrible place that makes our sons and daughters extremely worse than when they went into prison. No parent would discipline their children in such a cruel fashion. There has to be some kind of fairness and equity towards the troubled Americans that get ensnared in the system. Currently this country's media demonizes Americans that commit crime. This is done to dehumanize them. To stigmatize our country's sons and daughters so its easier to harshly and cruelly punish them according to what the prison special interests wants. Every time you see or listen to media outlets or pro-prison politicians speaking about rising crimes, sensationalizing particular crimes, demanding harsher laws, or fear-mongering, those are all dog whistles to incarcerate Americans sons and daughters. It is obvious and transparent to many Americans that mass incarceration is a plague on our country.

How do you end a plague? You recognize it and try to cure it. That's what we need to do with mass incarceration. Recognizing that warehousing Americans, stifling their identities and potential, denying them adequate treatments, keeping them uneducated, viciously oppressing and exploiting them, does not benefit the victims nor our society. Of course victims need to be a part of this conversation. Which is more than what the government gives victims in the current system. When you ask victims that had their car stolen, would you like to be compensated for your loss? Or to see the American that committed the crime incarcerated for five years? Most victims would take the money. The same goes for most crimes. Maybe there should be a monetary value for most crimes? In other words, if someone commits a crime they should be saddled with a debt that cannot be discharged into bankruptcy, like a student loan. Then they should be treated, educated, and allowed to begin their careers repaying the victims in the process. That simple innovation would significantly lower incarceration rates overnight! Opening up beds in the newly reimagined Treatment and Career Centers so that more money can be funnelled into rehabilitating those Americans that need treatment, education, and careers.

For property crimes that are fueled by the mental health problem of substance abuse disorder the person should be treated for drug addiction and trained for a job. If it is a more serious violent crime the person should be sentenced to treatment and a college degree. Whether its a AA Degree, Bachelors, Masters, or Doctorate Degree should depend upon the seriousness and/or repeated offense. That's how we should be looking at time structures for our American people. In treatment and educational degrees. Adequate treatments and educational degrees take time. Years. So sentencing troubled Americans in this fashion will work. It will discipline them, genuinely rehabilitate them, repair victims, and ultimately make them productive members of society. Even in the most advanced and civilized society there are gonna be those that need more treatment and time apart from society than others. The penalty for most crime should be under eight years, which is the amount of time needed to get a doctorate, with the maximum for the most egregious crimes at twenty years. Occassionally there are some crimes so heinous that they deserve longer sentences, such as serial killers and sociopaths, and those rare cases should get life sentences.

A country is judged by the way it treats the most vulnerable and voiceless populations in society. And our country treats those at the bottom, "criminals," terribly! Obviously it is a giant leap to jump from a punitive and cruel system to a fair and equitable system but many people are demanding it. It can be achieved. We must start with sentencing reform. Then prisons. Ultimately we could arrive at a system that treats Americans and releases them with degrees and/or careers! In my opinion that is not a high ask of a people from its government. Sure today these Americans are committing a crime, but tomorrow they could be a legislator or some other type of contributing member of society, therefore we are literally doing our society a disservice when we disregard these Americans based on a commission of crime. Criminality is not a permanent state of existence it is largely only a momentary lapse in civility based on one's mental health at that moment. Once we grasp that on a country wide basis we will finally realize our country's true potential.

In the Declaration of Independence the founders of our country declared that it was self-evident that all were created equal. If that is true then how can we treat our fellow Americans so badly once they have a momentary lapse due to a mental health disorder and end up in the criminal justice system? Its almost like we as a society are kicking a person when their already down. They are already struggling with poverty or mental health problems so adding warehousing in a violent and dangerous artificial environment is only making them worse. We know this by the data. It is clear as the blue sky. So why do we as a country continue to do it? It is because prison special interests have a vested interest in this cycle continuing and they have controlled the levers of power to keep it happening. Thankfully since the beginning of political systems there has been one power that can correct any injustice or inequity by the government and that's the power of the people! The people can unite behind reimagining prisons and make it happen.

CHAPTER TWO

LET US END ALL VESTIGES OF SLAVERY

For many Americans it would be outrageous to learn that slavery is alive and well in this country! Not only is it alive and well but it is a part of the U.S. Constitution. It is thriving! Which is repulsive to many people! We have to have a Constitutional Convention to end this cruel and inhumane practice. How can any civilized nation justify slavery? Let alone a nation which underwent a civil war to end the overt slavery of our African-American brethren. Now we have a hidden slavery that is destroying millions of Americans lives. No longer can Americans stand by and ignore the fact that our peoples are suffering in prisons and correctional complexes across this country.

Accordingly it is in the interests of all peoples to abolish slavery. In all its forms. Schools all across this country teach children about the horrors of slavery. Yet America is partaking in that horror on a daily basis. In every state imprisoned American's labor is being stolen from them. They are being forced to work for nothing or close to that. It is a disgrace. Is it far fetched to pay people minimum wage? No. It is not. If the government wants to TAKE any American's labor they can pay the prevailing wage. Those wages will help that American reentry into society. As it sits today governments release thousands of peoples with no funds accrued while incarcerated. Not only that but most times those Americans are saddled with vast amount of debt. As such thousands of Americans are being released untreated, uneducated, poor, and in debt. This is the status quo. How can anyone justify this injustice? They can't except by demonizing and fearmongering troubled souls that interact with the criminal justice system. By stating evilly that those that commit crime are not worthy of a fair wage. Just like those that justified slavery before the civil war.

For many Americans it would be a very easy sell to change the Constitution to abolish slavery. The problem may arise from the pro-prison media and pro-prison politicians though. In many media forums the whole proposition of ending slavery wouldn't even be allowed to show up in print. But we are living in a different age. With the advent of social media and other online resources we can go over the heads of these media outlets and pro-prison politicians. We can get the social justice message to the masses. Obviously it wouldn't be easy but it can be accomplished. Slavery has to be addressed. Without abolishing this ugly practice true advancement and progress will be hard to achieve.

There are not many arguments against ending slavery. That is because most civilized Americans would be repulsed by the notion that slavery still exists. Some might justify its existence since its only reserved to convicted felons. Yet such a rationalization is outdated. We are in a new era, a new culture is emerging that is diverse and hungry for equality and fairness for all peoples, even those convicted for a crime. It is extremely unfair that the government can STEAL peoples labor and then release those same people in poverty. Using slave labor to keep prisons running is a small piece of it. States also take slave labor to make State products such as licence plates, office supplies, and numerous other products to many to list. Beyond those State products they also take slave labor for private industrial companies. Regardless of how they steal incarcerated Americans' labor it is not justified and is repugnant to the values and mores of this changing country.

One of the most prevalent arguments against paying minimum wages for incarcerated Americans' labor is that the government would go broke. That argument is weak. First of all, if the government can constantly hand out unfairly long sentences, continue to build prisons unabated, and continue fostering this insane cycle of recitivism then they can afford to pay prevailing wages. The government wants citizens to think it would break their coffers if minimum wage was paid but that's just plain false. If all the reforms discussed in this book were implemented then government coffers would remain strong. Furthermore the fiscal argument against paying prevailing wages also smacks of hypocrisy. The government abolished slavery during the civil war despite this having an immense monetary impact on slave holders. Their fiscal loss was not powerful enough to keep the institution of slavery alive. Therefore it should not be enough of a powerful reason to keep slavery alive today.

The next argument used to maintain the institution of slavery today is that those peoples have committed felony crimes. This argument fails too. We are an advanced and civilized country so it is time we collectively step back from passions and prejudices to think what we want for our people moving forward. Do we want to yield our country's children to the government while it is seeing those children as slaves? Remember the statistic, one third of the American populace has been arrested, incarcerated, or put on probation. Within fifty years it will be two thirds. Do we want our progeny to be enslaved? If you don't, we have to stand together now. We can make a more perfect criminal justice system if we band together and demand change. To demand the abolishment of slavery. To stop stealing incarcerated Americans labor. Which will ensure those incarcerated Americans be released with enough funds to reenter into society.

Ending slavery does not merely assist the returning American and his family but rather it helps the entire community surrounding them. It ensures that incarcerated American can obtain housing, buy food, and contribute to his successful reintegration. Additionally with sufficient funds to return to society they will not immediately commit new crimes. As many Americans coming from the criminal justice system of today do.

Chapter Three

Repeal Victimless Crimes and All Enhancements

The biggest drain on governmental and societal resources is the prosecution of victimless crimes and their subsequent incarceration. Drug laws. Gun laws. Vice laws. They have gotten so ridiculously harsh and disproportionate that its outrageous and cruel. Vast amounts of Americans are being ensnared and enslaved in the criminal justice system for crazy amounts of years for victimless crimes. Relatively peaceful behavior is outlawed and pursued with the full force of the law. It is wrong. And outright stupid. Its not like the government has some magical power to change human behavior. The government is not making better citizens by incarcerating them for partaking in their choice of intoxicant, possessing a unlicensed firearm, or prostituting themselves. These victimless crimes, amongst many others, do not harm any one else, they do not infringe on any one else's pursuit of happiness, nor do they unduly burden society. Largely victimless crimes are peaceful and commerce driven. Criminalizing conduct that can rightly be defined as peaceful and commercial is despicable. It appears dirty and underhanded. As if those in power merely wanted another category of criminal code to enslave the American people. That is what it looks like in the trenches of mass incarceration. That's what it looks like to the millions of families, friends, and communities that are separated for years due to the prosecution of victimless crimes. It is impossible to view it any differently if you are woken to the struggle and educated on its vagrancies.

The drug laws are the most potent evidence of injustice and inequity. The moral compass of this country has got to point to a more lenient solution than incarcerating Americans for their choice of intoxicants. Drug laws are infringing on Americans pursuit of happiness on a grand scale. Our country should be increasing liberties not outlawing them. Who cares if one American choices heroin? Another choices cocaine? One marijuana? While the next picks beer, wine, or spirits? They are all inherently intoxicating substances. Sure some are more addictive and can cause deterioration more pronounced and quickly than others. Yet legalization for recreational use with heavy taxation can reap vast sums of money for health insurance for all Americans. Tax dollars could be used to fund health insurance that includes substance abuse treatment centers. That is one remedy that would produce considerable gains for all Americans. When I have this conversation with you I'm not speaking in a vacuum, I'm thinking about the methamphetamine user that puts a gram in her coffee before work every morning, goes back home at night to sleep, does it all over again the next morning, and has done it for twenty years.

The opioid user that has been using heroin for their back pain for years. Or the guy that likes to sniff a line of cocaine on the weekend at the bar/club. These are real Americans that are being ravished by criminalization of their intoxicant of choice. Its a human condition to self medicate or intoxicate oneself, since the beginning of human history, so outlawing them, encroaching on others pursuit of happiness is just plain wrong and needs to be changed.

The next most demonized category of victimless crimes is gun crimes. Most every person wants to be free from gun violence. No one wants that in their communities. However the legislatures, Federal and State, have gone bonkers over it. Their over sentencing Americans for unlawful gun possession is outrageous. Fifteen years for possession of a bullet. That's some of the laws out there. No one is harmed if an American exercises their right to bare arms. Its only when a violent crime occurs that it should be elevated to a higher degree. Unlawful possession of firearm shouldn't mean that American's life is basically over. That's ridiculously unfair and unjust. Gun possession without any victim should be treated as a civil infraction, with civil financial penalties. Not sending our Americans to be institutionalized for decades.

Just as bad is the invention of enhancements the legislatures are enamored by. Think of this, normally an American, such as myself, that commits an armed robbery gets the standard range of ten years, but due to arbitrary and capricious enhancement laws, that crime is elevated to thirty years. I walked away with a de facto death sentence! And so do millions of other Americans. Adding enhancements to basic sentences gives the government undue power to enslave and ensnare millions of more Americans moving forward. It is improper abuse of governmental power and we should all be disgusted by it. Repealing enhancement laws that are duplicative, harsh, and cruel should be important to all Americans.

The laws against vices: Prostitution. Gambling. Ect. Are another category of victimless crimes meant to criminalize normal human behaviors. These vices have been around since the beginning of time. It is nothing new under the sun. No one likes seeing someone prostitute themselves but they are only harming themselves and they are pursuing their happiness. The government should not abuse their power and encroach upon it. That should be a civil infraction, such as driving without a ticket, or other such harmless crimes. Peoples that do these crimes are merely struggling in our shared human story of life. Why penalize them with harsh unforgiving sentences that destroy them?

In many communities these crimes are hidden and under the radar but rest assured there are millions of Americans ensnared by them. We cannot look at these laws and the ensuing incarceration that follow as abstract ideas that will not affect us. No! They will affect all of us. And our next generations immensely. Increasing the rolls at prisons near you. While your family may escape incarceration today, tomorrow, or the next decade, someday the beast of mass incarceration will swallow them up.

Chapter Four

Restore Voting Rights To All Incarcerated Americans

One of the most effective ways to make a fair and just criminal justice system is by returning the right to vote. Disenfranchising our people so they are unable to vote is unacceptable. It leaves them powerless and voiceless. No wonder incarcerated Americans have been treated so badly for so long. If politicians had to solicit votes from those imprisoned they would know first hand the misery and neglect that occurs in prisons across this country. It is incumbent upon any advanced civil society to have free and unencumbered elections with all votes counted. That is not the case today in America. Millions of Americans are systematically silenced in the most harshest way imaginable. Through the voting box. It can not be a totally free society if it deprives any of its citizens the right to vote. The right to vote should not be fickle and dependent upon those in power to determine which peoples and communities should not be allowed to enter the voting box. All people should be permitted to cast a vote.

The last people that were systematically deprived of the right to vote were slaves and African Americans. That same ugly and disgusting practice is used today with incarcerated Americans and ex-felons. Those in power know the importance of the vote. They know the power the vote bestows upon the citizen. With voting rights all prisons across this beautiful country would be transformed overnight. Incarcerated Americans would be treated fairly. And if they weren't they would vote out the politicians that were willfully blind to their struggle. Its that simple. Yet some politician know this. So it is in their interest to keep this evil practice going. Of course not all politicians are against restoring voting rights. One state in particular, Vermont, has already rolled back their disenfranchisement laws. All their citizens are allowed to vote, even their incarcerated ones, and their society has not fallen apart. Therefore the notion that enfranchising incarcerated Americans and ex-felons will some how be bad for society is just plain false and wrong. Mainly it is a ploy used to keep peoples down.

One argument that is used to keep disenfranchisement laws intact is that it is a privilege to vote. I agree with that statement but I say its a privilege that is inalienable and should not be abridged by any law, rule, code, regulation, ect.. America has a democracy which bestows voting rights on its citizens from birth. It is our birthright to vote as Americans. No where in the Declaration of Independence or U.S. Constitution does it state imprisoned American and ex-felons forfeit their right to vote. It is about time we get to a place in this country when all citizens have the right to vote. Most people don't even know about this marginalization.

When I was rotting away in my prison cell I would recall thinking about voting rights. The thought arose when I heard about Vermont. How they allow all peoples of that State to vote. I remembered thinking how much better prison life would become for them once politicians had to pander for their votes. That's a fair system. A system based on equal representation in the people's legislature. That is needed. Paltry reforms meant to assuage the prison population into compliance and silence are not enough anymore. We the People should demand better for the Americans that come after us.

A society is always judged by the way they treat the most vulnerable, marginalized, and disenfranchised peoples in their society. Currently the most downtrodden and powerless population in America is those ensnared in the system of mass incarceration. Mass populations of peoples are suffering constant indignities by that system. They have zero voice in its repair or rebuilding. They are forced to sit powerlessly by as corrupt prison administrations exploit their family, friends, and communities for millions of dollars. They are wholly dependent upon those that abuse their power to act in their best interest. Such a self-interested system is by implication doomed to fail. Politicians will never see the error of their ways until the American People force them to see it. Which is possible when the vote is in the hands of the population they have currently subjugated.

The conscious of this country require a top to bottom examination of mass incarceration. Honest citizens witness the atrocity of recidivism. Incarcerated Americans are coming back to communities more criminalistic than when they went in! New victims are created within three years of release of millions of incarcerated Americans. It is not a fad. It is data. New lenient and rehabilitative measures are deeply needed. One huge step would be to allow incarcerated Americans the right to vote. Treating Americans as Americans is the answer. The biggest cause of recidivism is lack of treatment, funds, and careers. Yet those measures may never be adequately addressed unless voting rights are firmly in the hands of stakeholders. Incarcerated Americans, their families, friends, and communities are the stakeholders to a just and equitable system. So are good hearted Americans of all races, creeds, and religions. Together the bondage of the American people can be ended for all generations into the future. Let us be the generation that changed society for the better.

Obviously the experiment of mass incarceration has failed. That is evident by the data. Anyone with a half a brain can recognize failure when they see it. Look at every metric available that measures recidivism. Incarcerated Americans are getting out worse than when they went in. In general they are uneducated, poor, mentally disturbed, ignorant, and stuck in criminal cycle. To disrupt this cycle voting rights must be intact. Not only intact but flourishing as those rights will bestow the liberty of self determination and rehabilitation upon incarcerated Americans.

CHAPTER FIVE

ABOLISH OVER-SENTENCING!

The right amount of discipline to deter present and future crime has been studied at length. The proper dish of punishment to satisfy the victim's natural right to justice. While balancing the right to redemption and rehabilitation for the offending American. It should not be victim rights versus the troubled American's rights. But rather victim's rights balanced against the right of the Offender to be treated fairly and equitably by the government. Obviously some victims would like to see their offender beheaded, see their hands or arms cut off, or some other form of cruel punishment. But we are a civilized country with logical and rational people that can separate passions to ascertain the right amount of time. Most studies have proven that after seven years all rehabilitative measures cease to be effective. At that point it becomes cruel. Accordingly, every crime, besides murder, should carry no more than eight years. Eight years gives the Federal and State government their labor, energy, and bodies. While separating those Americans from their communities as they are treated, educated, and ultimately returned as productive members. Instead of returning them worse than when they went into prison. As it sits now, incarcerated Americans are more likely to create new victims within three years than they are to create a small business. That's disgusting. How can that be? It is due to the disproportionality of over sentencing amongst other factors. Please don't take my twenty year incarceration and think I was rehabilitated by the government. That wasn't the case. Instead I had to toil and struggle for my self redemption. The proper sentence for my crime, armed robbery, and most other violent crimes where no one dies, is eight years or less. Period. Any more than that and we are merely cruelly warehousing our people. When people ask my perspective on sentences for sex offenders, I am conflicted, on the one hand, I know first hand the devastating affects sex abuse causes, due to some deviants that abused me during childhood, see my book "Hopeless in Seattle: A Fosterkid's Manifesto," while on the other hand, I understand the human condition, how people can be troubled and need treatment. So yes, even these Americans should not get sentences longer than eight years.

The bigger picture is that most who interact with the criminal justice system are merely troubled Americans first and foremost! As troubled Americans they are travailing in the struggle of life just like everyone else. It may take some treatment, education, and career building to shape them into productive members of society but it will be worth it. America is a land that believes in second, third, and even fourth chances. It believes in the human capacity to change and reform. The underdog to triumph over past troubles. To become the full productive American they were meant to be. Therefore we must structure our sentences to reflect a more rational and logical purpose: (i) Redemption, (ii) rehabilitation, and (iii) reentry should be the sole purpose of all sentences. Anything else is abhorrent to this country's consciousness.

There are some exceptions, murderers, they are particularly troubled Americans. They need the most treatment and educational efforts. Therefore a sentence maxed out at twenty years should be reserved for each murder. Each body should be an additional twenty years. It is offensive to all people to lose family and friends. Therefore a more severe discipline is needed to rehabilitate them. That is fair. And compensatory. However, mitigating factors should always be considered fairly based on both sides of the Americans rights to life, liberty, and the pursuit of happiness. Victims and offending Americans rights should be weighed equally. Equality under the law. The fact of the matter we are all destined to die. Some die before others. As my best friend Doug died stabbed on an abandoned house's floor, when I was sixteen, that tragic story is detailed in "Hopeless In Seattle: A Street kid's Manifesto," (part two of the trilogy). Life is not promised tomorrow. We must worry about those here and now. That is paramount. So discipline must be proportionate.

In the ever changing struggle for a more perfect union. It has become readily apparent that the culture is changing in this country. Diverse populations familiar with past atrocities and oppression of the democratic and republican governments know that its time to get equity for both sides of the court table. Prosecution and Defendant. That its time we increase liberties and rights for all people. Allowing the government to enslave our children and our children's children. The cycles must end. Over sentencing Americans to long sentences is inhumane, uncivilized, unfair, and cruel. We can recognize the humanity in the humans by keeping most sentences under eight years. That is reasonable and fair.

Furthermore, it would vastly increase local, state, and federal coffers by immense amounts. Any fiscal hawk, Republican or Democrat, should be swayed by the savings from the long term caging and warehousing of Americans. As a libertarian I am neutral between the Republican and Democratic governments so I can speak clearly and with clean hands about the injustice inherent with over sentencing Americans. That eight years should be maximum discipline for most crimes including violent ones. And murders should be topped off at twenty years. All three strike laws should be abolished forthwith. All those are is death sentences anyways. Killing an American for stealing a slice of pizza is incredibly barbaric yet it is being done. It is disgusting and cruel. Three strike law is evil and wicked. The people that thought it up were operating on a inhumane and demonic level of human consciousness. They surely were not operating on a heart abundant with love for this country and its generations of peoples. That's for sure.

CHAPTER SIX

STOP ALL FORMS OF EXPLOITATION

Captive consumers! Forced customers! Those are the operative words. Private and Public prison profiteers are extracting vast millions, potential billions, from incarcerated Americans, their families, friends, and communities! Those extracted resources belong with them. Not fat cat elites that profit off misery, captivity, and injustice. Most everything costs money in prison: phone calls, emails, video visits, media, commissary, food packages, property packages, medical copays, and even hygiene. They all cost exorbitant amounts. Yet incarcerated Americans are paid nothing or nearly nothing. Therefore these costs are passed off to family and friends. They are saddled with the burden. Additionally some States, such as Washington, even go so far as to extort families and friends further by deducting a percentage of all incoming funds. Families and friends that work hard for their funds, which are taxed according to their tax brackets, are again taxed when they care for their loved one. How exploitative is that! Extremely.

    Phone calls, emails, media, and video visits are a big exploitative racket in prisons across this country. Big conglomerates charge exorbitantly high fees to access these resources. Phone calls are ridiculously expensive. They charge upward of two or three dollars per phone call. Imagine if you are striving to stay connected with your family or friends by calling frequently. This is a common thing inside. Incarcerated Americans use the phone all day long. Literally. Some will be on the phone from when they wake up to when they go to sleep. That is extremely expensive as each call is limited to twenty minutes. So every twenty minutes they are spending two or three dollars. As you can imagine that adds up quickly. Some are spending five hundred a week or more. That is immensely prohibitory. Many can not afford even one phone call. So they can go years sometimes without being able to call their family and friends. It is extremely sad. Yet it is completely fixable. First thing that needs to happen is end all kickbacks! Many of these prison phone companies have profit sharing agreements with the government so they are incentivised to continue this extortionate practice. End kickback profit sharing! Make phone calls free or close to free so that relationships can be strengthened and endure the hardship of separation. Phones should be integrated into tablets so incarcerated Americans can have uninhibited access. As far as emails and video visits they should likewise be free or nearly free. Currently a email costs a little less than a postage stamp costs to mail a regular envelope. Video visits can cost anywhere from twelve to thirteen dollars. These costs are burdensome. Many studies and data sets have proven that increasing connections with families, friends, and communities reduces recidivism significantly. To me that is common sense. We should do everything possible to renew and strengthen bonds to the family, friends, and communities that incarcerated Americans are ultimately going back to. The myriad of costs and fees charged are an effective wedge to building, renewing, or strengthening any relationships. There is no justification worthy enough to continue murdering these Americans relationships.

All taxes on incarcerated Americans incoming funds should be repealed. These taxes are exessively punitive. They are essentially extracting scarce funds from poor people. Many incarcerated Americans and their families fought valiantly in the courts to end this practice. Yet the courts always ruled with the government. No surprise there. So it appears we can only end this practice by popular demand. Again we must go over the heads of pro-prison special interests to demand change. The arguments against taxing incoming funds were numerous. One of them stemmed around double taxation, another was taxing the spouses household. Both are valid arguments yet they were denied by the courts. When families and friends sue the State to stop extorting them it is bad.

A current practice is allowing families and friends to buy property and food products from websites which would be delivered to the incarcerated American. This is all well and good until you examine the prices and products. The price of almost every product is ten times as much as a similar product would cost in the free world. That is plain wrong. Adding insult to this unfair practice is the fact that all the products are junk. It is junk food and junk property. Most the foods are high in sodium or unhealthy altogether. The property products such as TVs, radios, hotpots, typewriters, ect., are inadequately built and do not last long. If they were a private company selling goods to regular free world consumers they would be sued for unfair business practices but because they are selling their wares to incarcerated Americans they get away with it. That is despicable.

Due to the high level of recidivism it is important that we implement measures that actually work. We know through studies and data, and common sense, that healthy relationships with families, friends, and communities, will reduce reoffending so it is time we start strengthening them. Anything else would be foolhardy. Yet it will be a hard battle getting entrenched prison profiteers to stop the exploitation. Particularly if the government is getting kickbacks through profit sharing agreements. Highlighting the unfair business practices in the light of public examination and demands may make a substanial impact. Litigation through the courts was unsuccessful so we cannot rely on the judiciary. In my experience the judiciary rules almost exclusively in the favor of the government. Accordingly I believe we need to start protesting and advocating for ending all forms of exploitation within the criminal justice system. Maybe that is asking a lot but ending mass incarceration is extremely important!

Chapter Seven

Abolish All Forms of Oppression

Systemically oppressing incarcerated Americans has to stop. The militarization of corrections needs to end! We need to return to a place of sanity. It is insane to treat fellow Americans the way they are now. Incarcerated Americans are treated so badly and inhumanely it should be a crime in itself. Animals in shelters are treated better. It is a sickening plague. The myriad of petty rules. The trainings and teachings meant to degrade, debase, and demean incarcerated Americans. The abuses of power. The guard brutalities. The endless harassment and belittlement. The psychological operations and warfare of the mind to intellectually subjugate incarcerated Americans. All these atrocious practices have to end!

Inside prisons across this country there is a secret and hidden insidious effort to keep incarcerated Americans entangled in the system of mass incarceration. One of the ways to do that is by creating vast amounts of petty rules and regulations. Each time someone turns around they are stepping in some regulatory pothole or landmine. This is not by accident. It is by design. Rarely do incarcerated Americans make it through imprisonment without losing vast amounts of good time or being severely punished. Most of these violations are for relatively minor infractions which are inherent in communal living. They need to be reigned in. Unless the rule or regulation is for rehabilitative or safety purposes they should be abolished. Period. And that goes for all the petty rules associated with parole, probation, community custody, ect.. Those forms of control are meant to assure successful reentry into the community. But they have been transformed into pipelines to keep prisons stocked. Let us get to a place where these forms of control are doing what they are intended for, keeping Americans free and integrated into society.

The biggest misconception that many have when reading my books is that I'm anti-correctional officer. I'm not. I believe there's a job to be done keeping some incarcerated Americans inside, even if they were turned into treatment and career centers. The problem I have is with the trainings and educationing of correctional officers. Their trainings have evolved to a nefarious place. To assume everyone is a threat, a scammer, or a enemy, is a evil and dangerous place to be. That ensures maltreatment of those they interact with. But that could change relatively easily if trainings were redesigned to be less confrontational, violent, and superior. Most correctional officers will tell you strait up that they're trained to assume all inmates are liars, hustlers, violent, and manipulative. Those prejudices instill deep distrust and chill any genuine peaceful interactions with incarcerated Americans. These trainings ensure that correctional officers view incarcerated Americans as a population to ruthlessly control. This needs to stop. Trainings of correctional officers should be independently examined by stakeholders. Friends, family, ex-incarcerated Americans, and their associated communities should be indispensable resources to shape rehabilitative focused curriculum and trainings. The days of imposing force and coercion on incarcerated Americans has to end. Guard brutality has invaded the culture of most correctional institutions. That stems from their harsh and prejudicial trainings meant to dehumanize our fellow Americans.

Abuse of power is rampant in correctional facilities. Corrupt prison authorities and administrators are the rule not the exception. They view their job is to further their and their co-workers interests not the incarcerated American's. That breeds corruption. It ensures that the administration is beholden to correctional officers unions before the wellbeing and rehabilitation of those they are paid to care for. That is wrong. Honestly correctional officer unions are in itself an abuse. They focus solely on furthering their constituency's interests. How can such a organization exist in a system designed to rehabilitate? It can't. Prison authorities and administrators should be solely beholden to society and those they are paid to care for. Not their own interests or those of unions.

Psychological operations and intellectual subjugation is a real threat to incarcerated Americans. Stripping them of their clothes, identity, creativity, and personalities, is occurring on a mass scale. At virtually every prison they mandate uniforms or clothing that strips away individuality. All people want to be themselves. They want to be comfortable and feel unique. The current practice of uniform attire psychologically makes incarcerated Americans feel insignificant and stifled. This should end. Obviously some attire is needed for those without resources to obtain their own personal clothing but besides that incarcerated Americans should be allowed to wear regular clothes. Further psychologically damaging is the stifling of creativity. In prison any semblance of it is sought out and suppressed. For instance, tattooing, a common and acceptable career in the free world, is systematically suppressed. That is wrong. Further examples are too numerous to list herein. The fact is, we should be encouraging creativity, free thinking, and innovation, just like most colleges and universities across this country encourage it. If schools of higher education teach these attributes then why is it banished in prisons? Is it because the current purpose is to keep incarcerated Americans mentally subjugated and recidivising? If that's the purpose they are doing a flawless job at that. Yet if their intent is to end recidivism then we need to unchain our fellow Americans! We need to place the mental tools necessary to succeed in their hands without reservation. If they become free thinking, creative, and innovative individuals then a prison may produce the next Einstein, Tesla, Bezos, Steve Jobs, or Bill Gates!

Chapter Eight

Mandate Mental Health Treatment to End Recidivism

It may sound like elementary thinking to assert many entering prison are struggling with some form of mental health disorders. Substance abuse disorder. Post traumatic stress disorder. Depressive thought disorder. Delusion thought disorder. Ect.. The disorders are vast. But the treatments are not. In prison there is inadequate treatment solutions. Which is absurd. This should be a staple of prisons but largely it goes ignored. Why this is is unclear. I try to have non-conspiritorial thinking, however, it is worrisome that such a truth exists. It is occurring. There is a solution. And it is very apparent to most educated folks. One of the main focuses of prisons should be to provide mental treatment solutions and tools so that incarcerated Americans can release mentally intact and prepared to assimilate back into society. However that is not happening now. It seems the only purpose now is to keep incarcerated

Americans as troubled as they were when they came in so they promptly return within a few years. It is extremely counter intuitive to the mission statements of all correctional systems.

Every State and Federal prison should be transformed into treatment facilities! This could happen relatively easily. The political will must be there but other than that the facilities can be converted quickly. Mental health professionals could be hired. New methodologies could be created to treat masses amounts of Americans effectively. Obviously the workbooks and treatment solutions will have to evolve organically. But for the most part, we could all benefit as a society if this approach is put into place.

As a troubled incarcerated American myself, having been abandoned, rejected, and abused during childhood, see my book, "Hopeless in Seattle: A Fosterkid's Manifesto," to read the full extend of my suffering, I can state with one hundred percent certainty that treatment would of prevented years of criminality. Believe me, I am not unique. Many imprisoned Americans are suffering from some type of trauma that propelled their mental health deterioration. This much is clear and evident upon examination. It may cost on the front end, but on the back end we will be saving massive amounts of dollars.

The correctional systems should be entirely focused on treatment. Upon arrival at any facility those men or women should be examined and diagnosed forthwith. Upon diagnosis they should be transfered to the facility that specializes on that disorder. Mental health professionals, assistants, associates, and nurses should be amongst the population. They should not be hidden in dark offices estranged from their charges. How can that be effective. It can't. So its time they get in the trenches. To intermingle with those they treat so that effective understanding of each patient's needs are met. This is ideal. It is possible. And can be achieved if open-minded innovative approaches are tried.

As a consumer of American history I know there were periods of time when mental health was cared for. When mental institutions were prolific. Yet even those were not as effective as they could of been. Currently mental health has been criminalized as the prison system is the default setting for those with mental health disorders. We can all agree the prison system has not done a good job of treating them. So it is time to refocus energies on bettering our people. Leaving them in a better condition than when they enter the prison system. That will only be done if we invest time, funds, and sweat into them. Treating them like fellow Americans that will soon live next door to you. As the vast majority will be in your communities. This the only solution a civilized nation can choice.

As it is today, the criminal justice spends three times as much more on guns, bullets, weapons, fences, security systems, and other defensive and offensive measures, than they spend on bettering our countrymen that happen to be incarcerated. How can that be? How did we get to this juncture is unclear. But what is absolutely clear is the trend needs to reversed. We cannot continue down this road of misery, captivity, and recidivism.

There are many mental health solutions we can explore. Such as the method that places the drug of choice within arms length of the substance abuse patient, then training them to turn the drug down, over and over and over again. This creates new synapses and neurological pathways in the brain accustomed to rejecting the drug. Building up the fortitude and tenacity to live a long and prosperous life without substances. This is just one of many treatment options and solutions. Whether it would work on a mass scale is murky. But at least we would be attempting to better our people ridding them of their substance abuse disorder.

Let us take a moment to address the illusion of treatment. Each prison currently has some type of mental health treatment yet they are wholly inadequate and not effective. None of them seem to have made a dent in treating Americans and sending them out into society a better person. Not one. So please do not fall victim to current pro-prison special interests alleging that there are already treatment solutions. As there isn't any effective ones that I know of. Let us be clear, I am not stating that current mental health practitioners are ineffective themselves, but I am stating that the totality of the data regarding recidivism has proven that what is being done in criminal justice system is not working and has failed.

We need more mental health professionals to create, curate, and implement the next generation of the criminal justice system turning prisons into treatment centers. Let's hope that they answer the clarion call and come rushing to treat their fellow Americans. Otherwise this insane cycle of oppression, exploitation, and recidivism will continue unabatedly forever into the future.

Chapter Nine

Mandate Education and Careers to End Recidivism

Producing productive members of society upon their release should of been the goal of the criminal justice system. Sure they have used those words quite frequently throughout the years. But it has been lip service. They have not actually put in the work or provided the tools and education to meet this goal. We the people should not put up with such dereliction of duties. It is time to bring the light of education and careers back to the incarcerated people of this country. We can easily do this. And not with vast amounts of governmental funds either. Any free world citizen can easily apply and be approved for governmental educational loans. Those same funds are currently being unlocked again for incarcerated Americans. Once the full panoply of educational loans and grants are unveiled for the incarcerated American we might be able to take a step forward.

When I discuss my dreams and hopes for future generations of incarcerated Americans many people snicker and laugh at them. Such high ideals as degrees in microbiology, astrophysics, psychology, criminal justice, even medical doctorates! How audacious! A little of my story, after almost twenty years of incarceration I have gotten virtually zero formal education the entire time. My last grade of education was the sixth. I received a General Equivalency Degree ("GED") while in prison in 2000 but besides that my formal education is non-existence. That does not mean I am uneducated. I am self-educated. Truly. Books such as Blacks Law Dictionary, courtroom rule books, english books, and many others to numerous to list herein I read from front to back. Those books provided freedom of my mind. Even though my body was incarcerated and kept oppressed, exploited, and harassed. To expand your mind is to open your eyes. And my eyes are wide open.

We have many roads to the destination we seek. Can existing buildings within prisons handle the task of educating diverse courses and degrees? Maybe. But I don't think so. The best solution is busing to local colleges and Universities. If we are keeping all sentences at or below eight years the risk of escape diminishes significantly. So that shouldn't be a major objection or concern. Furloughs have been around for years. So is using prisoner labor in the community. Therefore the proposition of busing incarcerated Americans to local colleges and universities is more feasible than some might think.

Another solution could be satellites colleges and universities within existing facilities. They could educate the vast majority of incarcerated Americans within the prison walls. Many will need basic college level math, English, ect., so these courses could be taught within the prisons. I believe the more advanced the courses are the more likely outside furloughs might be called for. The logistics and design of formally educating incarcerated Americans might be an obstacle at some facilities. But it can happen.

Another thing that should be considered is that not all incarcerated Americans are monolithic. Some might not want to be educated with a college degree but might rather learn a trade. For instance, they may want to become welders, tattoo artists, marijuana growers, home builders, ect.. There needs to be diverse educational offerings so that incarcerated Americans can be all they want to be. The last thing we want to do is only offer cookie cutter degrees that don't adequately address different peoples needs and wants.

Thankfully recently the government has reversed the years long prohibition against federal aid for prisoners seeking to educate themselves. That is a great step forward. Now we need to use those dollars to widely expand education offerings. We can make the next generation smarter and less inclined to commit new crimes. That will be possible if we don't give up on them. I feel that's exactly what happened in the past. Largely due to racist "super predator" propaganda spewed by past politicians. But we are at the precipice of a new era. A new diverse and enlightened people are emerging demanding an end to the failed mass incarceration system. One way to do that is by educating incarcerated Americans with careers. There is a distinction between providing basic education and providing careers. When we speak of careers, I'm speaking about life long and secure work, in fields not going obsolete any time soon.

I believe in my heart the most important thing we can do for our people is to educate them and give them the tools to succeed. There will be such a low recidivism rate if all incarcerated Americans are released with degrees and career pathways. I cannot imagine someone releasing with a Bachelor's in Computer Science reoffending within three years. Even thinking about it sounds bizarre. I'm sure there will be some troubled souls that fall back into substance abuse but they will be more mature and knowledgable about how to control their disorder with the treatments they had gotten. So their risk of long term caging reduces significantly. Those beds that were once filled with returning Americans will now be open for the younger generation to get treated and educated. The cycle can be broken for recidivism. It will be a remarkable feat. One that many countries might point to for their prison reform efforts someday. Currently many people point to Denmark's criminal justice system and how humane it is. I wish that same attribute for my country and its people. I hope we get there in my lifetime. But if we don't at least I will know I had spent hours, days, and months writing and expressing my point of view. Maybe some future generation will take these writings and get inspiration from them. That is a another hope of mine. As time unfolds it will testify to the righteousness of educating our people. It will stand as a testament to future generations that keeping an imprisoned people in ignorance is inhumane, unjust, and wrong!

CHAPTER TEN

TEAR DOWN PRISON WALLS AND BEGIN SOCIALIZATION EFFORTS

Just because we have done something for a long time does not mean we have to continue doing it forever into the future! We can reimagine corrections! We can innovate! The proposition of tearing down prison walls and fences might sound infeasible and unworkable to some pro-prison special interests. But the fact is, if they keep sentences reasonable and fair, around eight years or less, the average incarcerated American will stay their stint and do their time getting the treatment and education they desperately need. Most will be pragmatic about their incarceration, viewing it as a time to better themselves and elevate their families, friends, and communities through their education and careers. We need to get past the notion that separating families, friends, and communities is somehow conducive for justice and rehabilitation efforts for the incarcerated American. Because that is not the case. In fact it seems contrary to the evidence. The data and evidence testifies that socialization might be the most effective rehabilitative and restorative measure we could use.

Many dreamers and innovators have the same dilemma! How do they get their ideas accepted by others. Depending on the idea it may be harder. Sometimes leading others to new innovations is not enough. That may be the case with this book. Regardless we have to put ourselves out there to change the status quo. With that said, I've got some crazy ideas to share with you. Largely what is said about those that commit crimes is that they are exhibiting "antisocial" behavior. So with that said, our ultimate goal should be to "socialize" them. Right? Okay. We agree on that premise. If that premise is true then why are prisons so inherently antisocial environments? Why do we keep incarcerated Americans completely separated from society? Is it because we always have? Well that's not a good enough answer. Sure we should separate offending Americans from society to some extent by housing them in refashioned prisons made into treatment and career centers. But while they are housed there can't they be trusted to socialize with their families, friends, and communities inhibited? Yes they can!

Let us throw out some crazy ideas! All the prison walls and fences should be taken down. The families, friends, and communities of incarcerated Americans should be able to walk the grounds and cells of prisons for daily visits. The wives and children should be allowed to live inside the cell with their loved ones as they are treated and educated. Incarcerated Americans should be able to buy smart phones, laptops, and tablets with unrestricted access to the internet. There should be dances where men and women from the community can come in to have fun with incarcerated Americans. There should be a market where incarcerated Americans can sell their creative goods (i.e. drawings, models, jewelry, ect.). The list of socialization efforts are endless! Yet what they all have in common is that their designed to keep families, friends, and communities together. This current corrupt mass incarceration system is quite the opposite!

When I spoke about tearing down prison walls and fences, I speak mainly about the facilities housing those with eight years or less. The optimal amount of time for rehabilitative purposes. If someone is in for longer than that maybe they should be housed at a facility with more of a secure perimeter. But other than that we should be focused on socialization!

Having families, friends, and communities walking amongst the incarcerated population would be hugely beneficial. It would ensure that incarcerated Americans maintain their societal connections. Strengthening them immensely. Incarcerated Americans will be focused on treatment and education while at the same time growing bonds with society. Having wives and children live with their loved one inside the prison would have the same socialization effect. Keep in mind, we want these people to become productive members of society! Therefore can you imagine how productive these incarcerated Americans would be if they were treated so humanely. Honestly who would you rather move in next door to you? A person confined in the current corrupt, oppressive, and exploitative system? Or a person in the herein discussed system? I mean really? Is there any doubt? It seems so obvious to me and many other Americans! We have to continue to strive for a more perfect union, reimaging the criminal justice system is one small piece of that. Can you imagine how many future American lives this system would save?

Allowing incarcerated Americans to purchase smartphones, laptops, and tablets, amongst other technologies, is a huge step forward. Not only will this encourage socialization but it will also obviate the current corrupt practice of gouging and extracting funds from incarcerated Americans, their families, friends, and communities. Can you imagine a day when your loved one can post Facebook messages and pictures from within their prison cell? It can happen. We just need to refocus on genuine rehabilitation again. Not applying lip service to it.

It is extremely important to have community functions such as dances and markets for obvious reasons. They will keep incarcerated Americans civilized and focused on advancing legitimate commerce. We need more of that inside the prisons across the country. In regards to dances, I can picture a single person meeting someone special during their period of incarcerated and getting married potentially having children. All while being treated and gaining a education and career. That is ultimate socialization. This incarcerated American would release with a family! Amazing! The criminal justice system would be engaged in genuine socialization and rehabilitation at this point. That is what we all want. These solutions are within reach and doable. We the people must demand them!

CHAPTER ELEVEN

END SOLITARY CONFINEMENT, DIESEL TREATMENT, AND CELL INSECURITY

As we embark on an authentic inventory of the current practices in use across this country in the mass incarceration system we must examine solitary confinement, diesel treatment, and cell insecurity. These forms of control are widely used and abused across this country. They are extremely damaging. And cause immense disruption in the incarcerated American's life. We must end all practices that worsen the mental health of our people. And these practices definitively do that. There is no disputing the trauma once it is examined. Therefore stepping back and discussing smarter ways to keep our people confined is the best solution.

Some States have seen the error of the torturous policy of solitary confinement but many haven't. Keep in mind this is a practice that has been defined in the United Nations Geneva Conventions as torture! Yet it is done on a mass scale and without apology across the country. It is absurd. As someone that has spent years in solitary confinement I can attest to the severe damage it caused me. In one particular stint of a year in solitary confinement I started hallucinating, hearing the theme song for "The Brady Bunch" tv show. Yep, I heard it in my vent. It would be funny if it wasn't so sad. That only happened in one stint of solitary confinement. Keep in mind, a free thinker and libertarian as I am, I was constantly being put in solitary confinement. In fact, my infraction history is pretty atrocious. Many of the infractions were for such things as tattooing, those that have seen me know I'm covered in tattooes, or petty offenses of marijuana usage, or befriending female correctional officers. Over a twenty year period I racked up close to eighty infractions. So trust me when I state I have experienced the vagrancies of solitary confinement. It is dangerous. Extremely damaging. And always made me worse than when I went in. Virtually every single human being I met that did a significant amount of solitary confinement time was mentally damaged afterwards. Every one. Without exceptions. That kind of incontrovertible data is compelling for most people. But not the pro-prison special interests groups. They minimize and excuse the torture as a way to control incarcerated Americans. It is repulsive and wrong. We must stop it.

Diesel treatment for the uninitiated means the frequent and unnecessary transfer of incarcerated Americans to different prisons throughout the State or country. This practice is used widely within almost every State and Federal system. It is extremely harmful and onerous for the incarcerated American. As you can imagine this practice causes immense disruption and hassle. Each time the incarcerated American is given diesel treatment they have to pay for their property to be shipped, they have to establish themselves amongst a new population, and get accustomed to a new environment. It is terrible. Believe me, I have experienced this harsh treatment many times. Washington has numerous prisons but the ones classified for those with more than five years are numbered at six. I have been transfered to every one of those six prisons. Sometimes more than once. So I can testify truthfully of the hardship. It was very disorienting and taxing on me. As it is with the millions of other incarcerated Americans dealing with it. We should keep incarcerated Americans at the closest facility to their communities of origin and not move them except for emergency purposes.

Another mentally damaging practice is known as cell insecurity. This is where the prison administration moves an incarcerated American within the prison from one cell to another, or one Unit to another, over and over again. They use this practice for many reasons. To punish. To deter. Because they don't like you. Or merely due to your political outspokeness! The pretexts are limitless. Yet the effects are the same. The incarcerated American suffers mentally. It is outrageous. Again, I have been on the brunt end of this practice many times, like so many times I cannot count. Imagine having to take down pictures of your loved ones, pack up all your property, say goodbye to your cellmate you may have befriended, move to a different cell or Unit and unpack all your property to restart the process of establishing yourself amongst the population again. This process is restarted over and over again ad nauseam! The discomfort and stress of it is immeasurable. This has to end. Incarcerated Americans should be securely housed in one cell or Unit and not moved unless there are valid reasons or emergency purposes.

The above are real threats to the mental health of our people. We have to endeavor to keep our people healthy mentally, educationally, and physically. The status quo of doing whatever administrators deem fit should finish. The interests of incarcerated American's health, safety, and rehabilitation should be the paramount concern. Administrators are people too, they are bound to make mistakes, to think of their own interests, and disregard the interests of the incarcerated American. That much is clear from examining how extremely harsh, rigid, and cold prisons are across this country. The pro-prison special interests have had control of the mass incarceration system long enough. Its time to bring humanity and heart back into the criminal justice system. It is evident that without change we will continue to collectively reap what we sow. And we are sowing mentally troubled Americans back into society to revictimize others, it is a vicious cycle, and will continue ad nauseam forever unless we reimagine a better solution. One that does not demonize and vilify troubled Americans but instead looks to treat and educate them so they can become productive members of society. We can reach this solution if we fight for it. We should truly strive for it because it is a just and fair reimagining.

Conclusion

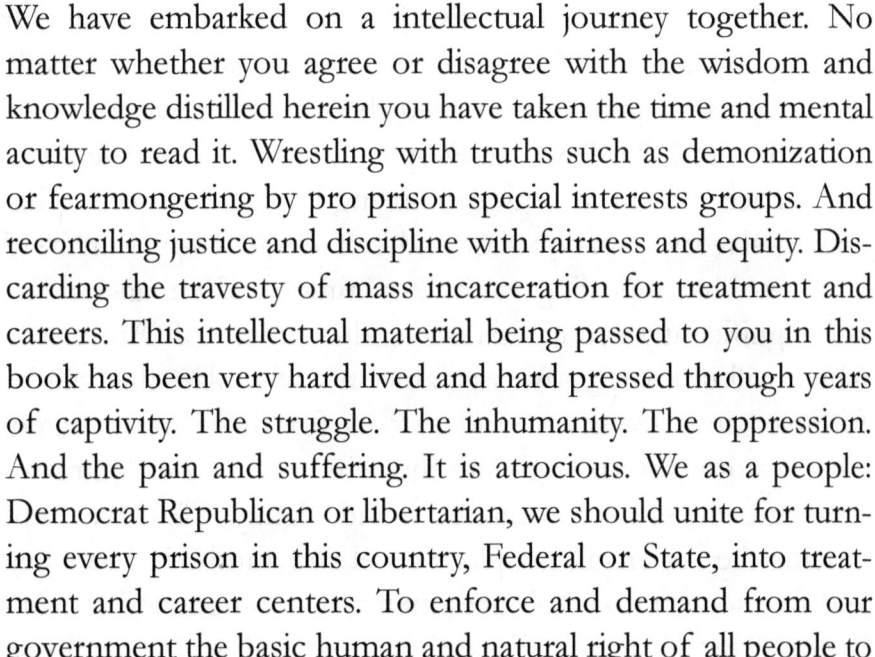

We have embarked on a intellectual journey together. No matter whether you agree or disagree with the wisdom and knowledge distilled herein you have taken the time and mental acuity to read it. Wrestling with truths such as demonization or fearmongering by pro prison special interests groups. And reconciling justice and discipline with fairness and equity. Discarding the travesty of mass incarceration for treatment and careers. This intellectual material being passed to you in this book has been very hard lived and hard pressed through years of captivity. The struggle. The inhumanity. The oppression. And the pain and suffering. It is atrocious. We as a people: Democrat Republican or libertarian, we should unite for turning every prison in this country, Federal or State, into treatment and career centers. To enforce and demand from our government the basic human and natural right of all people to be treated fairly and with dignity. The American people from coast to coast must unite for genuine reform to happen but it can happen. There are many solutions to this plague. We can cure the chronic ailment. Will you sit idly by as your fellow countrymen are enslaved and oppressed by the millions? Or will you stand firm on the conviction that America should be a country that embraces change and vote according to your good conscious. Regardless how you sit on the political fence, you must agree in the fundamental sanctity of human life. Do your children, or you children's children, deserve to be treated and educated when they enter mass incarceration? Because the way it is going they will interact with it someday. So shouldn't we begin striving now to make a more perfect solution for the crime and recidivism problem? We must resist ideologies that view troubled Americans as worthless criminals unworthy of restoration and rehabilitation.

As we conclude this treatise it is important to recap our journey. To ascertain the truths we heard. As such let us briefly discuss past chapters. We learned that discipline without love is tyranny and that "We the People" must demand true criminal justice reform in both sentencing laws and prisons. That ending slavery is paramount and self evident for a civilized country. That repealing victimless crimes and enhancements will significantly reduce arrests and captivity of Americans which will ultimately save vast amounts of dollars that can be funneled into treatment and careers for those incarcerated. That restoring voting rights to those incarcerated will improve transparency, self determination, and dignity. That over sentencing the American people is cruel and antithetical to a just and free society that embraces mercy, restoration, and rehabilitation. That all forms of extortion, extraction, and exploitation of incarcerated Americans and their families, friends, and communities must be rejected and ended. That abolishing the insidious forms of oppression rampant in today's mass incarceration system is the only answer for a fair and justice minded civic society. That mental health treatment, education, and careers have to be instituted upon our incarcerated people so that we can end this vicious cycle of recidivism. That tearing down prison walls and fences and beginning to socialize our incarcerated Americans will increase public safety and ultimately reduce recidivism. That any humane and just society must end the mentally damaging practices of solitary confinement, diesel treatment, and cell insecurity as they merely exacerbate incarcerated American's health.

This examination, dissection, and attending potential solution are expressed to rid this country of the plague of mass incarceration, recidivism, and the intergenerational captivity of our fellow Americans. To save our children and our children's children ad nauseam into the future from the misery, neglect, oppression, exploitation, and the lack of treatment and education that is solidified in the current corrupted system of mass incarceration.

Please take a minute and join the many grassroots movements that seek to advance our country and reform the criminal justice system for our descendants. You can further join my community online, my social media platforms, or my blogs to follow the arduous battle ahead. Regardless how you enlist in this effort your presence is incredibly crucial. Whether you are a Democrat, Republican, or a Libertarian such as I am, we should all want a more perfect criminal justice system!

Acknowledgment

I want to acknowledge all incarcerated people struggling in silent misery and despair. Whether they are white, black, hispanic, asian, or any other enthicity. All peoples engaged in educating themselves on the injustices occurring right under their noses in prisons across country. All peoples newly committed to taking action on reform, voting for reforms, and/or participating in the struggle for reform. Those are the people I acknowledge and thank. I recognize no family or friends as many have been willfully blind and deliberately indifferent to my pain and suffering and that of millions of other incarcerated Americans! I also want to acknowledge Victor Stephenson for his help editing. Charles "Walter" Weber for his invaluable input and suggestons, Tracy M. Simms for her immeasurable help throughout this publishing process, and Mike Stanton my fosterdad that stood by me though all these years.

APPENDIX A

THE DECLARATION OF INDEPENDENCE—1776
IN CONGRESS, JULY 4, 1776
The unanimous Declaration of the thirteen united States of America

WHEN in the Course of human events, it becomes necessary for one people to dissolve the political bands which have connected them with another, and to assume among the powers of the earth, the separate and equal station to which the Laws of Nature and of Nature's God entitle them, a decent respect to the opinions of mankind requires that they should declare the causes which impel them to the separation. We hold these truths to be self-evident, that all men are created equal, that they are endowed by their Creator with certain unalienable Rights, that among these are Life, Liberty and the pursuit of Happiness. That to secure these rights, Governments are instituted among Men, deriving their just powers from the consent of the governed,—That whenever any Form of

Government becomes destructive of these ends, it is the Right of the People to alter or to abolish it, and to institute new Government, laying its foundation on such principles and organizing its powers in such form, as to them shall seem most likely to effect their Safety and Happiness. Prudence, indeed, will dictate that Governments long established should not be changed for light and transient causes; and accordingly all experience hath shewn, that mankind are more disposed to suffer, while evils are sufferable, than to right themselves by abolishing the forms to which they are accustomed. But when a long train of abuses and usurpations, pursuing invariably the same Object evinces a design to reduce them under absolute Despotism, it is their right, it is their duty, to throw off such Government, and to provide new Guards for their future security.—Such has been the patient sufferance of these Colonies; and such is now the necessity which constrains them to alter their former Systems of Government. The history of the present King of Great Britain is a history of repeated injuries and usurpations, all having in direct object the establishment of an absolute Tyranny over these States. To prove this, let Facts be submitted to a candid world. He has refused his Assent to Laws, the most wholesome and necessary for the public good. He has forbidden his Governors to pass Laws of immediate and pressing importance, unless suspended in their operation till his Assent should be obtained; and when so suspended, he has utterly neglected to attend to them. He has refused to pass other Laws for the accommodation of large districts of people, unless those people would relinquish the right of Representation in the Legislature, a right inestimable to them and formidable to tyrants only. He has called together legislative bodies at places unusual, uncomfortable, and distance from the depository of their public Records, for the sole purpose of fatiguing them into compliance with his measures. He has dissolved Representative Houses repeatedly, for opposing with manly firmness his invasions on the rights of the people. He has refused for a long time, after such dissolutions, to cause others to be elected; whereby the Legislative powers, incapable of Annihilation, have returned to the People at large for their exercise; the State remaining in the mean time exposed to all the dangers of invasion from without, and convulsions within. He has endeavoured to prevent the population of these States; for that purpose obstructing the Laws for Naturalization of Foreigners; refusing to pass others to encourage their migrations hither, and raising the conditions of new Appropriations of Lands. He has obstructed the Administration of Justice, by refusing his Assent to Laws for establishing Judiciary powers. He has made Judges dependent on his Will alone, for the tenure of their offices, and the amount and payment of their salaries. He has erected a multitude of New Offices, and sent hither swarms of Officers to harass our people, and eat out their substance. He has kept among us, in times of peace, Standing Armies without the Consent of our legislatures. He has affected to render the Military independent of and superior to the Civil power. He has combined with others to subject us to a jurisdiction foreign to our constitution, and unacknowledged by our laws; giving his Assent to their acts of pretended Legislation: For quartering large bodies of armed troops among us: For protecting them, by a mock Trial, from punishment for any Murders which they should commit on the Inhabitants of these States: For cutting off our Trade with all parts of the world: For imposing Taxes on us without our Consent: For depriving us in many cases, of the benefits of Trial by Jury: For transporting us beyond Seas to be tried for pretended offenses: For abolishing the free System of English Laws in a neighbouring Province, establishing therein an Arbitrary government, and enlarging its Boundaries so as to render it at once an example and fit instrument for introducing the same absolute rule into these Colonies: For taking away our Charters, abolishing our most valuable Laws, and altering fundamentally the Forms of our Governments: For suspending our own Legislatures, and declaring themselves invested with power to legislate for us in all cases whatsoever. He has abdicated Government here, by declaring us out of his Protection and waging War against us. He has plundered our seas, ravaged our Coasts, burnt our towns, and destroyed the lives of our people. He is at this time transporting large Armies of foreign Mercenaries to compleat the works of death, desolation and tyranny, already begun with circumstances of Cruelty & perfidy scarcely paralleled in the most barbarous ages, and totally unworthy the Head of a civilized nation. He has constrained our fellow Citizens taken Captive on the high Seas to bear Arms against their Country, to become the executioners of their friends and Brethren, or to fall themselves by their Hands. He has excited domestic insurrections amongst us, and has endeavoured to bring on the inhabitants of our frontiers, the merciless Indian Savages, whose known rule of warfare, is an undistinguished destruction of all ages, sexes and conditions. In every stage of these Oppressions We have Petitioned for Redress in the most humble terms: Our repeated Petitions have been answered only by repeated injury. A Prince, whose character is thus marked by every act which may define a Tyrant, is unfit to be the ruler of a free people. Nor have We been wanting in attentions to our Brittish brethren. We have warned them from time to time of attempts by their legislature to extend an unwarrantable jurisdiction over us. We have reminded them of the circumstances of our emigration and settlement here. We have appealed to their native justice and magnanimity, and we have conjured them by the ties of our common kindred to disavow these usurpations, which, would inevitably interrupt our connections and correspondence. They too have been deaf to the voice of justice and of consanguinity. We must, therefore, acquiesce in the necessity, which denounces our Separation, and hold them, as we hold the rest of mankind, Enemies in War, in Peace Friends. WE, THEREFORE, the Representatives of the UNITED STATES OF AMERICA, in General Congress, Assembled, appealing to the Supreme Judge of the world for the rectitude of our intentions, do, in the Name, and by Authority of the good People of these Colonies, solemnly publish and declare, That these United Colonies are, and of Right ought to be FREE AND INDEPENDENT STATES; that they are Absolved from all Allegiance to the British Crown, and that all political connection between them and the State of Great Britain, is and ought to be totally dissolved; and that as Free and Independent States, they have full Power to levy War, conclude Peace, contract Alliances, establish Commerce, and to do all other Acts and Things which Independent States may of right do. And for the support of this Declaration, with a firm reliance on the protection of divine Providence, we mutually pledge to each other our Lives, our Fortunes and our sacred Honor.

JOHN HANCOCK. New Hampshire JOSIAH BARTLETT, MATTHEW THORNTON. WM. WHIPPLE, Massachusetts Bay SAML. ADAMS, ROBT. TREAT PAINE, JOHN ADAMS, ELBRIDGE GERRY. Rhode Island STEP. HOPKINS, WILLIAM ELLERY. Connecticut ROGER SHERMAN, WM. WILLIAMS, SAM'EL HUNTINGTON, OLIVER WOLCOTT. New York WM. FLOYD, FRANS. LEWIS, PHIL. LIVINGSTON, LEWIS MORRIS. New Jersey RICHD. STOCKTON, JOHN HART, JNO. WITHERSPOON, ABRA. CLARK. FRAS. HOPKINSON, Pennsylvania ROBT. MORRIS, JAS. SMITH, BENJAMIN RUSH, GEO. TAYLOR, BENJA. FRANKLIN, JAMES WILSON, JOHN MORTON, GEO. ROSS. GEO. CLYMER, Delaware CAESAR RODNEY, THO. M'KEAN. GEO. READ, Maryland SAMUEL CHASE, CHARLES CARROLL OF WM. PACA, Carrollton. THOS. STONE, Virginia GEORGE WYTHE, THOS. NELSON, jr., RICHARD HENRY LEE, FRANCIS LIGHTFOOT TH. JEFFERSON, LEE, BENJA. HARRISON, CARTER BRAXTON. North Carolina WM. HOOPER, JOHN PENN. JOSEPH HEWES, South Carolina THOS. HEYWARD, Junr., THOMAS LYNCH, Junr., ARTHUR MIDDLETON. EDWARD RUTLEDGE, Georgia BUTTON GWINNETT, GEO. WALTON. LYMAN HALL,

NOTE.—Mr. Ferdinand Jefferson, Keeper of the Rolls in the Department of State, at Washington, says: "The names of the signers are spelt above as in the facsimile of the original, but the punctuation of them is not always the same; neither do the names of the States appear in the facsimile of the original. The names of the signers of each State are grouped together in the fac-simile of the original, except the name of Matthew Thornton, which follows that of Oliver Wolcott."

1The delegates of the United Colonies of New Hampshire; Massachusetts Bay; Rhode Island and Providence Plantations; Connecticut; New York; New Jersey; Pennsylvania; New Castle, Kent, and Sussex, in Delaware; Maryland; Virginia; North Carolina, and South Carolina, In Congress assembled at Philadelphia, Resolved on the 10th of May, 1776, to recommend to the respective assemblies and conventions of the United Colonies, where no government sufficient to the exigencies of their affairs had been established, to adopt such a government as should, in the opinion of the representatives of the people, best conduce to the happiness and safety of their constituents in particular, and of America in general. A preamble to this resolution, agreed to on the 15th of May, stated the intention to be totally to suppress the exercise of every kind of authority under the British crown. On the 7th of June, certain resolutions respecting independency were moved and seconded. On the 10th of June it was resolved, that a committee should be appointed to prepare a declaration to the following effect: "That the United Colonies are, and of right ought to be, free and independent States; that they are absolved from all allegiance to the British crown; and that all political connection between them and the State of Great Britain is, and ought to be, totally dissolved." On the preceding day it was determined that the committee for preparing the declaration should consist of five, and they were chosen accordingly, in the following order: Mr. Jefferson, Mr. J. Adams, Mr. Franklin, Mr. Sherman, Mr. R. R. Livingston. On the 11th of June a resolution was passed to appoint a committee to prepare and digest the form of a confederation to be entered into between the colonies, and another committee to prepare a plan of treaties to be proposed to foreign powers. On the 12th of June, it was resolved, that a committee of Congress should be appointed by the name of a board of war and ordnance, to consist of five members. On the 25th of June, a declaration of the deputies of Pennsylvania, met in provincial conference, expressing their willingness to concur in a vote declaring the United Colonies free and independent States, was laid before Congress and read. On the 28th of June, the committee appointed to prepare a declaration of independence brought in a draught, which was read, and ordered to lie on the table. On the 1st of July, a resolution of the convention of Maryland, passed the 28th of June, authorizing the deputies of that colony to concur in declaring the United Colonies free and independent States, was laid before Congress and read. On the same day Congress resolved itself into a committee of the whole, to take into consideration the resolution respecting independency. On the 2d of July, a resolution declaring the colonies free and independent States, was adopted. A declaration to that effect was, on the same and the following days, taken into further consideration. Finally, on the 4th of July, the Declaration of Independence was agreed to, engrossed on paper, signed by John Hancock as president, and directed to be sent to the several assemblies, conventions, and committees, or councils of safety, and to the several commanding officers of the continental troops, and to be proclaimed in each of the United States, and at the head of the Army. It was also ordered to be entered upon the Journals of Congress, and on the 2d of August, a copy engrossed on parchment was signed by all but one of the fiftysix signers whose names are appended to it. That one was Matthew Thornton, of New Hampshire, who on taking his seat in November asked and obtained the privilege of signing it. Several who signed it on the 2d of August were absent when it was adopted on the 4th of July, but, approving of it, they thus signified their approbation.

NOTE.—The proof of this document, as published above, was read by

Mr. Ferdinand Jefferson, the Keeper of the Rolls at the Department of State, at Washington, who compared it with the fac-simile of the original in his custody. He says: "In the facsimile, as in the original, the whole instrument runs on without a break, but dashes are mostly inserted. I have, in this copy, followed the arrangement of paragraphs adopted in the publication of the Declaration in the newspaper of John Dunlap, and as printed by him for the Congress, which printed copy is inserted in the original Journal of the old Congress. The same paragraphs are also made by the author, in the original draught preserved in the Department of State."

APPENDIX B

THE CONSTITUTION

of the United States

We the People of the United States, in Order to form a more perfect Union, establish Justice, insure domestic Tranquility, provide for the common defence, promote the general Welfare, and secure the Blessings of Liberty to ourselves and our Posterity, do ordain and establish this Constitution for the United States of America

Article. I.

SECTION. 1

All legislative Powers herein granted shall be vested in a Congress of the United States, which shall consist of a Senate and House of Representatives.

SECTION. 2

The House of Representatives shall be composed of Members chosen every second Year by the People of the several States, and the Electors in each State shall have the Qualifications requisite for Electors of the most numerous Branch of the State Legislature.

No Person shall be a Representative who shall not have attained to the Age of twenty five Years, and been seven Years a Citizen of the United States, and who shall not, when elected, be an Inhabitant of that State in which he shall be chosen.[Representatives and direct Taxes shall be apportioned among the several States which may be included within this Union, according to their respective Numbers, which shall be determined by adding to the whole Number of free Persons, including those bound to Service for a Term of Years, and excluding Indians not taxed, three fifths of all other Persons.]* The actual Enumeration shall be made within three Years after the first Meeting of the Congress of the United States, and within every subsequent Term of ten Years, in such Manner as they shall by Law direct. The Number of Representatives shall not exceed one for every thirty Thousand, but each State shall have at Least one Representative; and until such enumeration shall be made, the State of New Hampshire shall be entitled to chuse three, Massachusetts eight, Rhode Island and Providence Plantations one, Connecticut five, New-York six, New Jersey four, Pennsylvania eight, Delaware one, Maryland six, Virginia ten, North Carolina five, South Carolina five, and Georgia three. When vacancies happen in the Representation from any State, the Executive Authority thereof shall issue Writs of Election to fill such Vacancies.

The House of Representatives shall chuse their Speaker and other Officers; and shall have the sole Power of Impeachment.

SECTION. 3

The Senate of the United States shall be composed of two Senators from each State, [chosen by the Legislature there of,]* for six Years; and each Senator shall have one Vote.

Immediately after they shall be assembled in Consequence of the first Election, they shall be divided as equally as may be into three Classes. The Seats of the Senators of the first Class shall be vacated at the Expiration of the second Year, of the second Class at the Expiration of the fourth Year, and of the third Class at the Expiration of the sixth Year, so that one third may be chosen every second Year; [and if Vacancies happen by Resignation, or otherwise, during the Recess of the Legislature of any State, the Executive thereof may make temporary Appointments until the next Meeting of the Legislature, which shall then fill such Vacancies.]*

No Person shall be a Senator who shall not have attained to the Age of thirty Years, and been nine Years a Citizen of the United States, and who shall not, when elected, be an Inhabitant of that State for which he shall be chosenThe Vice President of the United States shall be President of the Senate, but shall have no Vote, unless they be equally divided. The Senate shall chuse their other Officers, and also a President pro tempore, in the Absence of the Vice President, or when he shall exercise the Office of President of the United States. The Senate shall have the sole Power to try all Impeachments. When sitting for that Purpose, they shall be on Oath or Affirmation. When the President of the United States is tried, the Chief Justice shall preside: And no Person shall be convicted without the Concurrence of two thirds of the Members present.Judgment in Cases of Impeachment shall not extend further than to removal from Office, and disqualification to hold and enjoy any Office of honor, Trust or Profit under the United States: but the Party convicted shall nevertheless be liable and subject to Indictment, Trial, Judgment and Punishment, according to Law.

SECTION. 4

The Times, Places and Manner of holding Elections for Senators and Representatives, shall be prescribed in each State by the Legislature thereof; but the Congress may at any time by Law make or alter such Regulations, except as to the Places of chusing Senators. The Congress shall assemble at least once in every Year, and such Meeting shall be [on the first Monday in December,]* unless they shall by Law appoint a different Day.

SECTION. 5.

Each House shall be the Judge of the Elections, Returns and Qualifications of its own Members, and a Majority of each shall constitute a Quorum to do Business; but a smaller Number may adjourn from day to day, and may be authorized to compel the Attendance of absent Members, in such Manner, and under such Penalties as each House may provide. Each House may determine the Rules of its Proceedings, punish its Members for disorderly Behaviour, and, with the Concurrence of two thirds, expel a Member.

Each House shall keep a Journal of its Proceedings, and from time to time publish the same, excepting such Parts as may in their Judgment require Secrecy; and the Yeas and Nays of the Members of either House on any question shall, at the Desire of one fifth of those Present, be entered on the Journal. Neither House, during the Session of Congress, shall, without the Consent of the other, adjourn for more than three days, nor to any other Place than that in which the two Houses shall be sitting.

SECTION. 6

The Senators and Representatives shall receive a Compensation for their Services, to be ascertained by Law, and paid out of the Treasury of the United States. They shall in all Cases, except Treason, Felony and Breach of the Peace, be privileged from Arrest during their Attendance at the

Session of their respective Houses, and in going to and returning from the same; and for any Speech or Debate in either House, they shall not be questioned in any other Place. No Senator or Representative shall, during the Time for which he was elected, be appointed to any civil Office under the Authority of the United States, which shall have been created, or the Emoluments whereof shall have been encreased during such time; and no Person holding any Office under the United States, shall be a Member of either House during his Continuance in Office.

SECTION. 7

All Bills for raising Revenue shall originate in the House of Representatives; but the Senate may propose or concur with Amendments as on other BillsEvery Bill which shall have passed the House of Representatives and the Senate, shall, before it become a Law, be presented to the President of the United States; If he approve he shall sign it, but if not he shall return it, with his Objections to that House in which it shall have originated, who shall enter the Objections at large on their Journal, and proceed to reconsider it. If after such Reconsideration two thirds of that House shall agree to pass the Bill, it shall be sent, together with the Objections, to the other House, by which it shall likewise be reconsidered, and if approved by two thirds of that House, it shall become a Law. But in all such Cases the Votes of both Houses shall be determined by Yeas and Nays, and the Names of the Persons voting for and against the Bill shall be entered on the Journal of each House respectively, If any Bill shall not be returned by the President within ten Days (Sundays excepted) after it shall have been presented to him, the Same shall be a Law, in like Manner as if he had signed it, unless the Congress by their Adjournment prevent its Return, in which Case it shall not be a LawEvery Order, Resolution, or Vote to which the Concurrence of the Senate and House of Representatives may be necessary (except on a question of Adjournment) shall be presented to the President of the United States; and before the Same shall take Effect, shall be approved by him, or being disapproved by him, shall be repassed by two thirds of the Senate and House of Representatives, according to the Rules and Limitations prescribed in the Case of a Bill.

SECTION. 8

The Congress shall have Power To lay and collect Taxes, Duties, Imposts and Excises, to pay the Debts and provide for the common Defence and general Welfare of the United States; but all Duties, Imposts and Excises shall be uniform throughout the United States;To borrow Money on the credit of the United States; To regulate Commerce with foreign Nations, and among the several States, and with the Indian Tribes; To establish an uniform Rule of Naturalization, and uniform Laws on the subject of Bankruptcies throughout the United States; To coin Money, regulate the Value thereof, and of foreign Coin, and fix the Standard of Weights and Measures; To provide for the Punishment of counterfeiting the Securities and current Coin of the United States; To establish Post Offices and post Roads; To promote the Progress of Science and useful Arts, by securing for limited Times to Authors and Inventors the exclusive Right to their respective Writings and Discoveries; To constitute Tribunals inferior to the supreme Court; To define and punish Piracies and Felonies committed on the high Seas, and Offenses against the Law of Nations; To declare War, grant Letters of Marque and Reprisal, and make Rules concerning Captures on Land and Water; To raise and support Armies, but no Appropriation of Money to that Use shall be for a longer Term than two Years; To provide and maintain a Navy; To make Rules for the Government and Regulation of the land and naval Forces; To provide for calling forth the Militia to execute the Laws of the Union, suppress Insurrections and repel Invasions; To provide for organizing, arming, and disciplining, the Militia, and for governing such Part of them as may be employed in the Service of the United States, reserving to the States respectively, the Appointment of the Officers, and the Authority of training the Militia according to the discipline prescribed by Congress; To exercise exclusive Legislation in all Cases whatsoever, over such District (not exceeding ten Miles square) as may, by Cession of particular States, and the Acceptance of Congress, become the Seat of the Government of the United States, and to exercise like Authority over all Places purchased by the Consent of the Legislature of the State in which the Same shall be, for the Erection of Forts, Magazines, Arsenals, dock-Yards and other needful Buildings; And To make all Laws which shall be necessary and proper for carrying into Execution the foregoing Powers, and all other Powers vested by this Constitution in the Government of the United States, or in any Department or Officer thereof.

SECTION. 9

The Migration or Importation of such Persons as any of the States now existing shall think proper to admit, shall not be prohibited by the Congress prior to the Year one thousand eight hundred and eight, but a Tax or duty may be imposed on such Importation, not exceeding ten dollars for each Person The Privilege of the Writ of Habeas Corpus shall not be suspended, unless when in Cases of Rebellion or Invasion the public Safety may require it. No Bill of Attainder or ex post facto Law shall be passed. [No Capitation, or other direct, Tax shall be laid, unless in Proportion to the Census or Enumeration herein before directed to be taken.]*

No Tax or Duty shall be laid on Articles exported from any State

No Preference shall be given by any Regulation of Commerce or Revenue to the Ports of one State over those of another: nor shall Vessels bound to, or from, one State, be obliged to enter, clear, or pay Duties in another. No Money shall be drawn from the Treasury, but in Consequence of Appropriations made by Law; and a regular Statement and Account of the Receipts and Expenditures of all public Money shall be published from time to time. No Title of Nobility shall be granted by the United States: And no Person holding any Office of Profit or Trust under them, shall, without the Consent of the Congress, accept of any present, Emolument, Office, or Title, of any kind whatever, from any King, Prince, or foreign State.

SECTION. 10

No State shall enter into any Treaty, Alliance, or Confederation; grant Letters of Marque and Reprisal; coin Money; emit Bills of Credit; make any Thing but gold and silver Coin a Tender in Payment of Debts; pass any Bill of Attainder, ex post facto Law, or Law impairing the Obligation of Contracts, or grant any Title of Nobility. No State shall, without the Consent of the Congress, lay any Imposts or Duties on Imports or Exports, except what may be absolutely necessary for executing it's inspection Laws: and the net Produce of all Duties and Imposts, laid by any State on Imports or Exports, shall be for the Use of the Treasury of the United States; and all such Laws shall be subject to the Revision and Controul of the Congress. No State shall, without the Consent of Congress, lay any Duty of Tonnage, keep Troops, or Ships of War in time of Peace, enter into any Agreement or Compact with another State, or with a foreign Power, or engage in War, unless actually invaded, or in such imminent Danger as will not admit of delay.

Article. II.

SECTION. 1

The executive Power shall be vested in a President of the United States of America. He shall hold his Office during the Term of four Years, and, together with the Vice President, chosen for the same Term, be elected, as follows:

Each State shall appoint, in such Manner as the Legislature thereof may direct, a Number of Electors, equal to the whole Number of Senators and Representatives to which the State may be entitled in the Congress: but no Senator or Representative, or Person holding an Office of Trust or Profit under the United States, shall be appointed an Elector. [The

Electors shall meet in their respective States, and vote by Ballot for two Persons, of whom one at least shall not be an Inhabitant of the same State with themselves. And they shall make a List of all the Persons voted for, and of the Number of Votes for each; which List they shall sign and certify, and transmit sealed to the Seat of the Government of the United States, directed to the President of the Senate. The President of the Senate shall, in the Presence of the Senate and House of Representatives, open all the Certificates, and the Votes shall then be counted. The Person having the greatest Number of votes shall be the President, if such Number be a Majority of the whole Number of Electors appointed; and if there be more than one who have such Majority, and have an equal Number of Votes, then the House of Representatives shall immediately chuse by Ballot one of them for President; and if no Person have a Majority, then from the five highest on the List the said House shall in like Manner chuse the President. But in chusing the President, the Votes shall be taken byStates, the Representation from each State having one Vote; A quorum for this Purpose shall consist of a Member or Members from two thirds of the States, and a Majority of all the States shall be necessary to a Choice. In every Case, after the Choice of the President, the Person having the greatest Number of Votes of the Electors shall be the Vice President. But if there should remain two or more who have equal Votes, the Senate shall chuse from them by Ballot the Vice President.]*

The Congress may determine the Time of chusing the Electors, and the Day on which they shall give their Votes; which Day shall be the same throughout the United States. No Person except a natural born Citizen, or a Citizen of the United States, at the time of the Adoption of this Constitution, shall be eligible to the Office of President; neither shall any person be eligible to that Office who shall not have attained to the Age of thirty five Years, and been fourteen Years a Resident within the United States. In Case of the Removal of the President from Office, or of his

Death, Resignation, or Inability to discharge the Powers and Duties of the said Office, the Same shall devolve on the Vice President, and the Congress may by Law provide for the Case of Removal, Death, Resignation or Inability, both of the President and Vice President, declaring what Officer shall then act as President, and such Officer shall act accordingly, until the Disability be removed, or a President shall be elected.]*

The President shall, at stated Times, receive for his Services, a Compensation, which shall neither be increased nor diminished during the Period for which he shall have been elected, and he shall not receive within that Period any other Emolument from the United States, or any of them. Before he enter on the Execution of his Office, he shall take the following Oath or Affirmation: "I do solemnly swear (or affirm) that I will faithfully execute the Office of President of the United States, and will to the best of my Ability, preserve, protect and defend the Constitution of the United States."

SECTION. 2

The President shall be Commander in Chief of the Army and Navy of the United States, and of the Militia of the several States, when called into the actual Service of the United States; he may require the Opinion, in writing, of the principal Officer in each of the executive Departments, upon any Subject relating to the Duties of their respective Offices, and he shall have Power to grant Reprieves and Pardons for Offenses against the United States, except in Cases of Impeachment.

He shall have Power, by and with the Advice and Consent of the Senate, to make Treaties, provided two thirds of the Senators present concur; and he shall nominate, and by and with the Advice and Consent of the Senate, shall appoint Ambassadors, other public Ministers and Consuls, Judges of the supreme Court, and all other Officers of the United States, whose Appointments are not herein otherwise provided for, and which shall be established by Law: but the Congress may by Law vest the Appointment of such inferior Officers, as they think proper, in the President alone, in the Courts of Law, or in the Heads of Departments. The President shall have Power to fill up all Vacancies that may happen during the Recess of the Senate, by granting Commissions which shall expire at the End of their next Session.

SECTION. 3

He shall from time to time give to the Congress Information of the State of the Union, and recommend to their Consideration such Measures as he shall judge necessary and expedient; he may, on extraordinary Occasions, convene both Houses, or either of them, and in Case of Disagreement between them, with Respect to the Time of Adjournment, he may adjourn them to such Time as he shall think proper; he shall receive Ambassadors and other public Ministers; he shall take Care that the Laws be faithfully executed, and shall Commission all the Officers of the United States.

SECTION. 4

The President, Vice President and all civil Officers of the United States, shall be removed from Office on Impeachment for, and Conviction of, Treason, Bribery, or other high Crimes and Misdemeanors.

Article. III.

SECTION. 1

The judicial Power of the United States, shall be vested in one supreme Court, and in such inferior Courts as the Congress may from time to time ordain and establish. The Judges, both of the supreme and inferior Courts, shall hold their Offices during good Behaviour, and shall at stated Times, receive for their Services, a Compensation, which shall not be diminished during their Continuance in Office.

SECTION. 2

The judicial Power shall extend to all Cases, in Law and Equity, arising under this Constitution, the Laws of the United States, and Treaties made, or which shall be made, under their Authority; to all Cases affecting Ambassadors, other public Ministers and Consuls; to all Cases of admiralty and maritime Jurisdiction; to Controversies to which the United States shall be a Party; to Controversies between two or more States; [between a State and Citizens of another State;]* between Citizens of different States, between Citizens of the same State claiming Lands under Grants of different States, [and between a State, or the Citizens thereof; and foreign States, Citizens or Subjects.]* In all Cases affecting Ambassadors, other public Ministers and Consuls, and those in which a State shall be Party, the supreme Court shall have original Jurisdiction. In all the other Cases before mentioned, the supreme Court shall have appellate Jurisdiction, both as to Law and Fact, with such Exceptions, and under such Regulations as the Congress shall make. The Trial of all Crimes, except in Cases of Impeachment; shall be by Jury; and such Trial shall be held in the State where the said Crimes shall have been committed; but when not committed within any State, the Trial shall be at such Place or Places as the Congress may by Law have directed.

SECTION. 3

Treason against the United States, shall consist only in levying War against them, or in adhering to their Enemies, giving them Aid and Comfort. No Person shall be convicted of Treason unless on the Testimony of two Witnesses to the same overt Act, or on Confession in open Court.

The Congress shall have Power to declare the Punishment of Treason, but no Attainder of Treason shall work Corruption of Blood, or Forfeiture except during the Life of the Person attainted.

Article. IV.

SECTION. 1

Full Faith and Credit shall be given in each State to the public Acts, Records, and judicial Proceedings of every other State. And the Congress may by general Laws prescribe the Manner in which such Acts, Records and Proceedings shall be proved, and the Effect thereof.

SECTION. 2

The Citizens of each State shall be entitled to all Privileges and Immunities of Citizens in the several StatesA Person charged in any State with Treason, Felony, or other Crime, who shall flee from Justice, and be found in another State, shall on Demand of the executive Authority of the State from which he fled, be delivered up, to be removed to the State having Jurisdiction of the Crime. No Person held to Service or Labour in one State, under the Laws thereof, escaping into another, shall, in Consequence of any Law or Regulation therein, be discharged from such Service or Labour, but shall be delivered up on Claim of the Party to whom such Service or Labour may be due.]*

SECTION. 3

New States may be admitted by the Congress into this Union; but no new State shall be formed or erected within the Jurisdiction of any other State; nor any State be formed by the Junction of two or more States, or Parts of States, without the Consent of the Legislatures of the States concerned as well as of the Congress.

The Congress shall have Power to dispose of and make all needful Rules and Regulations respecting the Territory or other Property belonging to the United States; and nothing in this Constitution shall be so construed as to Prejudice any Claims of the United States, or of any particular State.

SECTION. 4

The United States shall guarantee to every State in this Union a Republican Form of Government, and shall protect each of them against Invasion; and on Application of the Legislature, or of the Executive (when the Legislature cannot be convened) against domestic Violence.

Article. V.

The Congress, whenever two thirds of both Houses shall deem it necessary, shall propose Amendments to this Constitution, or, on the Application of the Legislatures of two thirds of the several States, shall call a Convention for proposing Amendments, which in either Case, shall be valid to all Intents and Purposes, as Part of this Constitution, when ratified by the Legislatures of three-fourths of the several States, or by Conventions in three fourths thereof, as the one or the other Mode of Ratification may be proposed by the Congress; Provided that no Amendment which may be made prior to the Year One thousand eight hundred and eight shall in any Manner affect the first and fourth Clauses in the Ninth Section of the first Article; and that no State, without its Consent, shall be deprived of its equal Suffrage in the Senate.

Article. VI.

All Debts contracted and Engagements entered into, before the Adoption of this Constitution, shall be as valid against the United States under this Constitution, as under the Confederation. This Constitution, and the Laws of the United States which shall be made in Pursuance thereof; and all Treaties made, or which shall be made, under the Authority of the United States, shall be the supreme Law of the Land; and the Judges in every State shall be bound thereby, any Thing in the Constitution or Laws of any State to the Contrary notwithstanding. The Senators and Representatives before mentioned, and the Members of the several State Legislatures, and all executive and judicial Officers, both of the United States and of the several States, shall be bound by Oath or Affirmation, to support this Constitution; but no religious Test shall ever be required as a Qualification to any Office or public Trust under the United States

Article. VII.

The Ratification of the Conventions of nine States, shall be sufficient for the Establishment of this Constitution between the States so ratifying the Same. Done in Convention by the Unanimous Consent of the States present the Seventeenth Day of September in the Year of our Lord one thousand seven hundred and Eighty seven and of the Independence of the United States of America the Twelfth In Witness whereof We have hereunto subscribed our Names, Go. Washington--Presidt: and deputy from Virginia

NEW HAMPSHIRE

John Langdon Nicholas Gilman

MASSACHUSETTS

Nathaniel Gorham Rufus King

CONNECTICUT

Wm. Saml. Johnson Roger Sherman

NEW YORK

Alexander Hamilton

NEW JERSEY

Wil: Livingston David Brearley Wm. Paterson Jona: Dayton

PENNSYLVANIA

B Franklin Thomas Mifflin Robt Morris Geo. Clymer Thos. FitzSimons Jared Ingersoll James Wilson

Gouv Morris

DELAWARE

Geo: Read Gunning Bedford jun John Dickinson Richard Bassett Jaco: Broom

MARYLAND

James McHenry

Dan of St. Thos. Jenifer Danl Carroll

VIRGINIA
John Blair-   James Madison Jr.
NORTH CAROLINA
Wm. Blount
Richd. Dobbs Spaight Hu Williamson
SOUTH CAROLINA
J. Rutledge
Charles Cotesworth Pinckney Charles Pinckney
Pierce Butler
GEORGIA
William Few Abr Baldwin

Attest William Jackson Secretary

In Convention Monday September 17th, 1787. Present The States of New Hampshire, Massachusetts, Connecticut, Mr. Hamilton from New York, New Jersey, Pennsylvania, Delaware, Maryland, Virginia, North Carolina, South Carolina and Georgia. Resolved, That the preceeding Constitution be laid before the United States in Congress assembled, and that it is the Opinion of this Convention, that it should afterwards be submitted to a Convention of Delegates, chosen in each State by the People thereof, under the Recommendation of its Legislature, for their Assent and Ratification; and that each Convention assenting to, and ratifying the Same, should give Notice thereof to the United States in Congress assembled. Resolved, That it is the Opinion of this Convention, that as soon as the Conventions of nine States shall have ratified this Constitution, the United States in Congress assembled should fix a Day on which Electors should be appointed by the States which shall have ratified the same, and a Day on which the Electors should assemble to vote for the President, and the Time and Place for commencing Proceedings under this Constitution. That after such Publication the Electors should be appointed, and the Senators and Representatives elected: That the Electors should meet on the Day fixed for the Election of the President, and should transmit their Votes certified, signed, sealed and directed, as the Constitution requires, to the Secretary of the United States in Congress assembled, that the Senators and Representatives should convene at the Time and Place assigned; that the Senators should appoint a President of the Senate, for the sole Purpose of receiving, opening and counting the Votes for President; and, that after he shall be chosen, the Congress, together with the President, should, without Delay, proceed to execute this Constitution.

By the unanimous Order of the Convention
Go. Washington-Presidt:
W. JACKSON Secretary.

Language in brackets has been changed by amendment.

THE AMENDMENTS TO THE CONSTITUTION OF THE UNITED STATES AS RATIFIED BY THE STATES

Preamble to the Bill of Rights
Congress of the United States begun and held at the City of New-York, on Wednesday the fourth of March,

THE Conventions of a number of the States, having at the time of their adopting the Constitution, expressed a desire, in order to prevent misconstruction or abuse of its powers, that further declaratory and restrictive clauses should be added: And as extending the ground of public confidence in the Government, will best ensure the beneficent ends of its institution.

RESOLVED by the Senate and House of Representatives of the United States of America, in Congress assembled, two thirds of both Houses concurring, that the following Articles be proposed to the Legislatures of the several States, as amendments to the Constitution of the United States, all, or any of which Articles, when ratified by three fourths of the said Legislatures, to be valid to all intents and purposes, as part of the said Constitution; viz.

ARTICLES in addition to, and Amendment of the Constitution of the United States of America, proposed by Congress, and ratified by the Legislatures of the several States, pursuant to the fifth Article of the original Constitution.

(Note: The first 10 amendments to the Constitution were ratified December 15, 1791, and form what is known as the "Bill of Rights.")

Amendment I.

Congress shall make no law respecting an establishment of religion, or prohibiting the free exercise thereof; or abridging the freedom of speech, or of the press, or the right of the people peaceably to assemble, and to petition the Government for a redress of grievances.

Amendment II.

A well regulated Militia, being necessary to the security of a free State, the right of the people to keep and bear Arms, shall not be infringed.

Amendment III.

No Soldier shall, in time of peace be quartered in any house, without the consent of the Owner, nor in time of war, but in a manner to be prescribed by law.

Amendment IV.

The right of the people to be secure in their persons, houses, papers, and effects, against unreasonable searches and seizures, shall not be violated, and no Warrants shall issue, but upon probable cause, supported by Oath or affirmation, and particularly describing the place to be searched, and the persons or things to be seized.

Amendment V.

No person shall be held to answer for a capital, or otherwise infamous crime, unless on a presentment or indictment of a Grand Jury, except in cases arising in the land or naval forces, or in the Militia, when in actual service in time of War or public danger; nor shall any person be subject for the same offence to be twice put in jeopardy of life or limb; nor shall be compelled in any criminal case to be a witness against himself, nor be deprived of life, liberty, or property, without due process of law; nor shall private property be taken for public use, without just compensation.

Amendment VI.

In all criminal prosecutions, the accused shall enjoy the right to a speedy and public trial, by an impartial jury of the State and district wherein the crime shall have been committed, which district shall have been previously ascertained by law, and to be informed of the nature and cause of the accusation; to be confronted with the witnesses against him; to have compulsory process for obtaining witnesses in his favor, and to have the Assistance of Counsel for his defence.

Amendment VII.

In suits at common law, where the value in controversy shall exceed twenty dollars, the right of trial by jury shall be preserved, and no fact tried by a jury shall be otherwise reexamined in any Court of the United States, than according to the rules of the common law.

Amendment VIII.

Excessive bail shall not be required, nor excessive fines imposed, nor cruel and unusual punishments inflicted.

Amendment IX.

The enumeration in the Constitution, of certain rights, shall not be construed to deny or disparage others retained by the people.

Amendment X.

The powers not delegated to the United States by the Constitution, nor prohibited by it to the States, are reserved to the States respectively, or to the people.

Amendment XI.

Passed by Congress March 4, 1794. Ratified February 7, 1795.

(Note: A portion of Article III, Section 2 of the Constitution was modified by the 11th Amendment.)

The Judicial power of the United States shall not be construed to extend to any suit in law or equity, commenced or prosecuted against one of the United States by Citizens of another State, or by Citizens or Subjects of any Foreign State.

Amendment XII.

Passed by Congress December 9, 1803. Ratified June 15, 1804.

(Note: A portion of Article II, Section 1 of the Constitution was changed by the 12th Amendment.)

The Electors shall meet in their respective states, and vote by ballot for President and Vice-President, one of whom, at least, shall not be an inhabitant of the same state with themselves; they shall name in their ballots the person voted for as President, and in distinct ballots the person voted for as Vice-President, and they shall make distinct lists of all persons voted for as President, and of all persons voted for as Vice-President, and of the number of votes for each, which lists they shall sign and certify, and transmit sealed to the seat of the government of the United States, directed to the President of the Senate; the President of the Senate shall, in the presence of the Senate and House of Representatives, open all the certificates and the votes shall then be counted;-The person having the greatest number of votes for President, shall be the President, if such number be a majority of the whole number of Electors appointed; and if no person have such majority, then from the persons having the highest numbers not exceeding three on the list of those voted for as President, the House of Representatives shall choose immediately, by ballot, the President. But in choosing the President, the votes shall be taken by states, the representation from each state having one vote; a quorum for this purpose shall consist of a member or members from two-thirds of the states, and a majority of all the states shall be necessary to a choice. [And if the House of Representatives shall not choose a President whenever the right of choice shall devolve upon them, before the fourth day of March next following, then the Vice-President shall act as President, as in case of the death or other constitutional disability of the President.]* The person having the greatest number of votes as Vice-President, shall be the Vice-President, if such number be a majority of the whole number of Electors appointed, and if no person have a majority, then from the two highest numbers on the list, the Senate shall choose the Vice-President; a quorum for the purpose shall consist of two-thirds of the whole number of Senators, and a majority of the whole number shall be necessary to a choice. But no person constitutionally ineligible to the office of President shall be eligible to that of Vice-President of the United States.

*Superseded by Section 3 of the 20th Amendment.

Amendment XIII.

Passed by Congress January 31, 1865. Ratified December 6, 1865.
(Note: A portion of Article IV, Section 2 of the Constitution was changed by the 13th Amendment.)

SECTION 1

Neither slavery nor involuntary servitude, except as a punishment for crime whereof the party shall have been duly convicted, shall exist within the United States, or any place subject to their jurisdiction.

SECTION 2

Congress shall have power to enforce this article by appropriate legislation.

Amendment XIV.

Passed by Congress June 13, 1866. Ratified July 9, 1868.
(Note: Article I, Section 2 of the Constitution was modified by Section 2 of the 14th Amendment.)

SECTION 1

All persons born or naturalized in the United States and subject to the jurisdiction thereof, are citizens of the United States and of the State wherein they reside. No State shall make or enforce any law which shall abridge the privileges or immunities of citizens of the United States; nor shall any State deprive any person of life, liberty, or property, without due process of law; nor deny to any person within its jurisdiction the equal protection of the laws.

SECTION 2

Representatives shall be apportioned among the several States according to their respective numbers, counting the whole number of persons in each State, excluding Indians not taxed. But when the right to vote at any election for the choice of electors for President and Vice President of the United States, Representatives in Congress, the Executive and Judicial officers of a State, or the members of the Legislature thereof, is denied to any of the male inhabitants of such State, [being twenty-one years of age,]* and citizens of the United States, or in any way abridged, except for participation in rebellion, or other crime, the basis of representation therein shall be reduced in the proportion which the number of such male citizens shall bear to the whole number of male citizens twenty-one years of age in such State.

SECTION 3

No person shall be a Senator or Representative in Congress, or elector of President and Vice President, or hold any office, civil or military, under the United States, or under any State, who, having previously taken an oath, as a member of Congress, or as an officer of the United States, or as a member of any State legislature, or as an executive or judicial officer of any State, to support the Constitution of the United States, shall have engaged in insurrection or rebellion against the same, or given aid or comfort to the enemies thereof. But Congress may by a vote of two-thirds of each House, remove such disability.

SECTION 4

The validity of the public debt of the United States, authorized by law, including debts incurred for payment of pensions and bounties for services in suppressing insurrection or rebellion, shall not be questioned. But neither the United States nor any State shall assume or pay any debt or obligation incurred in aid of insurrection or rebellion against the United States, or any claim for the loss or emancipation of any slave; but all such debts, obligations and claims shall be held illegal and void.

SECTION 5

The Congress shall have the power to enforce, by appropriate legislation, the provisions of this article.

*Changed by Section 1 of the 26th Amendment.

Amendment XV.

Passed by Congress February 26, 1869. Ratified February 3, 1870.

SECTION 1

The right of citizens of the United States to vote shall not be denied or abridged by the United

States or by any State on account of race, color, or previous condition of servitude.

SECTION 2

The Congress shall have the power to enforce this article by appropriate legislation.

Amendment XVI.

Passed by Congress July 2, 1909. Ratified February 3, 1913.

(Note: Article I, Section 9 of the Constitution was modified by the 16 h Amendment.)

The Congress shall have power to lay and collect taxes on incomes, from whatever source derived, without apportionment among the several States, and without regard to any census or enumeration.

Amendment XVII.

Passed by Congress May 13, 1912. Ratified April 8, 1913.

(Note: Article I, Section 3 of the Constitution was modified by the 17th Amendment.)

The Senate of the United States shall be composed of two Senators from each State, elected by the people thereof, for six years; and each Senator shall have one vote. The electors in each State shall have the qualifications requisite for electors of the most numerous branch of the State legislatures.

When vacancies happen in the representation of any State in the Senate, the executive authority of such State shall issue writs of election to fill such vacancies: Provided, That the legislature of any State may empower the executive thereof to make temporary appointments until the people fill the vacancies by election as the legislature may direct.

This amendment shall not be so construed as to affect the election or term of any Senator chosen before it becomes valid as part of the Constitution.

Amendment XVIII.

Passed by Congress December 18, 1917. Ratified January 16, 1919. Repealed by the 21 Amendment, December 5, 1933.

SECTION 1

After one year from the ratification of this article the manufacture, sale, or transportation of intoxicating liquors within, the importation thereof into, or the exportation thereof from the United States and all territory subject to the jurisdiction thereof for beverage purposes is hereby prohibited.

SECTION 2

The Congress and the several States shall have concurrent power to enforce this article by appropriate legislation.

SECTION 3

This article shall be inoperative unless it shall have been ratified as an amendment to the Constitution by the legislatures of the several States, as provided in the Constitution, within seven years from the date of the submission hereof to the States by the Congress.

Amendment XIX.

Passed by Congress June 4, 1919. Ratified August 18, 1920.

The right of citizens of the United States to vote shall not be denied or abridged by the United States or by any State on account of sex. Congress shall have power to enforce this article by appropriate legislation.

Amendment XX.

Passed by Congress March 2, 1932. Ratified January 23, 1933.

(Note: Article I, Section 4 of the Constitution was modified by Section 2 of this Amendment. In addition, a portion of the 12th Amendment was superseded by Section 3.)

SECTION 1

The terms of the President and the Vice President shall end at noon on the 20th day of January, and the terms of Senators and Representatives at noon on the 3d day of January, of the years in which such terms would have ended if this article had not been ratified; and the terms of their successors shall then begin.

SECTION 2

The Congress shall assemble at least once in every year, and such meeting shall begin at noon on the 3d day of January, unless they shall by law appoint a different day.

SECTION 3

If, at the time fixed for the beginning of the term of the President, the President elect shall have died, the Vice President elect shall become President. If a President shall not have been chosen before the time fixed for the beginning of his term, or if the President elect shall have failed to qualify, then the Vice President elect shall act as President until a President shall have qualified; and the Congress may by law provide for the case wherein neither a President elect nor a Vice President shall have qualified, declaring who shall then act as President, or the manner in which one who is to act shall be selected, and such person shall act accordingly until a President or Vice President shall have qualified.

SECTION 4

The Congress may by law provide for the case of the death of any of the persons from whom the House of Representatives may choose a President whenever the right of choice shall have devolved upon them, and for the case of the death of any of the persons from whom the Senate may choose a Vice President whenever the right of choice shall have devolved upon them.

SECTION 5

Sections 1 and 2 shall take effect on the 15th day of October following the ratification of this article.

SECTION 6

This article shall be inoperative unless it shall have been ratified as an amendment to the Constitution by the legislatures of three-fourths of the several States within seven years from the date of its submission.

Amendment XXI.

Passed by Congress February 20, 1933. Ratified December 5, 933.

SECTION 1

The eighteenth article of amendment to the Constitution of the United States is hereby repealed.

SECTION 2

The transportation or importation into any State, Territory, or possession of the United States for delivery or use therein of intoxicating liquors, in violation of the laws thereof, is hereby prohibited.

SECTION 3

This article shall be inoperative unless it shall have been ratified as an amendment to the Constitution by conventions in the several States, as provided in the Constitution, within seven years from the date of the submission hereof to the States by the Congress.

Amendment XXII.

Passed by Congress March 21, 1947. Ratified February 27, 951.

SECTION 1

No person shall be elected to the office of the President more than twice, and no person who has held the office of President, or acted as President, for more than two years of a term to which some other person was elected President shall be elected to the office of President more than once. But this Article shall not apply to any person holding the office of President when this Article was proposed by Congress, and shall not prevent any person who may be holding the office of President, or acting as President, during the term within which this Article becomes operative from holding the office of President or acting as President during the remainder of such term.

SECTION 2

This article shall be inoperative unless it shall have been ratified as an amendment to the Constitution by the legislatures of three-fourths of the several States within seven years from the date of its submission to the States by the Congress.

Amendment XXIII.

Passed by Congress June 16, 1960. Ratified March 29, 1961.

SECTION 1

The District constituting the seat of Government of the United States shall appoint in such manner as Congress may direct: A number of electors of President and Vice President equal to the whole number of Senators and Representatives in Congress to which the District would be entitled if it were a State, but in no event more than the least populous State; they shall be in addition to those appointed by the States, but they shall be considered, for the purposes of the election of President and Vice President, to be electors appointed by a State; and they shall meet in the District and perform such duties as provided by the twelfth article of amendment.

SECTION 2

The Congress shall have power to enforce this article by appropriate legislation.

Amendment XXIV.

Passed by Congress August 27, 1962. Ratified January 23, 1964.

SECTION 1

The right of citizens of the United States to vote in any primary or other election for President or Vice President, for electors for President or Vice President, or for Senator or Representative in Congress, shall not be denied or abridged by the United States or any State by reason of failure to pay poll tax or other tax.

SECTION 2

The Congress shall have power to enforce this article by appropriate legislation.

Amendment XXV.

Passed by Congress July 6, 1965. Ratified February 10, 1967.
(Note: Article II, Section 1 of the Constitution was modified by the 25th Amendment.)

SECTION 1

In case of the removal of the President from office or of his death or resignation, the Vice President shall become President.

SECTION 2

Whenever there is a vacancy in the office of the Vice President, the President shall nominate a Vice President who shall take office upon confirmation by a majority vote of both Houses of Congress.

SECTION 3

Whenever the President transmits to the President pro tempore of the Senate and the Speaker of the House of Representatives his written declaration that he is unable to discharge the powers and duties of his office, and until he transmits to them a written declaration to the contrary, such powers and duties shall be discharged by the Vice President as Acting President.

SECTION 4

Whenever the Vice President and a majority of either the principal officers of the executive departments or of such other body as Congress may by law provide, transmit to the President pro tempore of the Senate and the Speaker of the House of Representatives their written declaration that the President is unable to discharge the powers and duties of his office, the Vice President shall immediately assume the powers and duties of the office as Acting President.

Thereafter, when the President transmits to the President pro tempore of the Senate and the Speaker of the House of Representatives his written declaration that no inability exists, he shall resume the powers and duties of his office unless the Vice President and a majority of either the principal officers of the executive department or of such other body as Congress may by law provide, transmit within four days to the President pro tempore of the Senate and the Speaker of the House of Representatives their written declaration that the President is unable to discharge the powers and duties of his office. Thereupon Congress shall decide the issue, assembling within forty-eight hours for that purpose if not in session. If the Congress, within twenty-one days after receipt of the latter written declaration, or, if Congress is not in session, within twenty-one days after Congress is required to assemble, determines by two-thirds vote of both Houses that the

President is unable to discharge the powers and duties of his office, the Vice President shall continue to discharge the same as Acting President; otherwise, the President shall resume the powers and duties of his office.

Amendment XXVI.

Passed by Congress March 23, 1971. Ratified July 1, 1971.
(Note: Amendment 14, Section 2 of the Constitution was modified by Section 1 of the 26th Amendment.)

SECTION 1

The right of citizens of the United States, who are eighteen years of age or older, to vote shall not be denied or abridged by the United States or by any State on account of age.

SECTION 2

The Congress shall have power to enforce this article by appropriate legislation.

Amendment XXVII.

Originally proposed Sept. 25, 1789. Ratified May 7, 1992.

No law, varying the compensation for the services of the Senators and Representatives, shall take effect, until an election of representatives shall have intervened.

Defund DOC

Biography

Daniel Simms was born on October 2, 1980, at Northwest Hospital in Seattle. He is a born-again Christian who found his faith in a dark place. He has hopes and dreams that he is trying to achieve while he is incarcerated. In addition to his GED, he has also achieved his paralegal certificate. In his spare time, he likes to stay up-to-date with current events by reading as much as he can. He has a thirst for knowledge. He has one son, Dillon.

www.ingramcontent.com/pod-product-compliance
Lightning Source LLC
Chambersburg PA
CBHW071113030426
42336CB00013BA/2065